ONE WORLD ALMANAC 2022

We can, through our creativity and imagination, through our solidarity and interconnectedness, create a planetary freedom movement through which we break free of the chains and walls constructed by the illusions of the mechanical mind, the money machine and the delusion of democracy.

VANDANA SHIVA
INDIAN ENVIRONMENTAL ACTIVIST AND FOOD-SOVEREIGNTY ADVOCATE
(1952-)

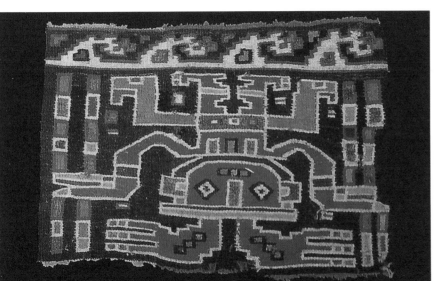

THIS ALMANAC BELONGS TO:

NAME

ADDRESS

TELEPHONE

MOBILE

EMAIL

YOUR SYMBOL FOR THE YEAR 2022:

This Peruvian textile figure was woven between 800 and 1000 CE. More ancient textiles have been found in Peru than anywhere else in the world. They survived because of their lavish use in burials – as much yarn was used to wrap a single mummy as for the clothing of several hundred living people.

MY 2022 ALMANAC INCLUDES

OUTSIDE FRONT COVER
YEARS 2022, 2023

INSIDE FRONT COVER
FULL-COLOUR WORLD MAP ON PETERS' PROJECTION

YEAR PLANNER
SIX MONTHS TO A DOUBLE PAGE

DIARY
ONE WEEK TO VIEW, JANUARY TO DECEMBER 2022

BACK PAGES
MORE BACKGROUND ON SOME OF THE ALMANAC PHOTOGRAPHS

NUMBER NUGGETS – KEY FACTS AND FIGURES

BIODIVERSITY LOSS AND HOW TO REVERSE IT

USEFUL WEBSITES

LAST THOUGHT

LAST SECTION
BLANK PAGES FOR ADDRESSES/NOTES

INSIDE BACK COVER
CONTACTS FOR THE ALMANAC PHOTOGRAPHERS

CAPTION FOR THE FRONT COVER PHOTOGRAPH

MIX
Paper from
responsible sources
FSC
www.fsc.org FSC® C016973

RELIGIOUS FESTIVALS 2022
(those where the date changes each year)

Buddhist
Visakha Puja   27 May

Chinese
Lunar New Year   1 February

Christian (Western)
Ash Wednesday   2 March
Good Friday   15 April
Easter Day   17 April
Ascension Day   26 May
First Sunday of Advent   27 November

Hindu
Vasant Panchami   5 February
Diwali begins   24 October

Jewish
Passover begins   15 April
Rosh Hashanah begins   25 September
Yom Kippur   4 October
Sukkot begins   9 October
Hanukkah begins   18 December

Muslim*
Ramadan begins   2 April
Eid al-Fitr   2 May
Ashura   7 August
Mawlid al-Nabi (Sunni)   8 October
Mawlid al-Nabi (Shia)   12 October

*Dates subject to visibility of new moon at Mecca

MOON PHASES

New moon 🌑 First quarter 🌓 Full moon 🌕 Last quarter 🌗
The moon phases are marked in the scale of universal time (UT) also called Greenwich Mean Time (GMT).

It is the standard time of the Greenwich Meridian (0 degrees of longitude). The time in UT may be converted to local mean time by the addition of the degrees of east longitude (or subtraction of west longitude), where the longitude of the place is expressed in time-measure at the rate of 1 hour for every 15 degrees. Local clock time may differ from standard, especially in summer when clocks are often advanced 1 hour.

DIARY PUBLIC HOLIDAYS AND FESTIVALS
Public holidays in the English-speaking countries where most users of this Almanac live are included, together with selected international days and festivals.

Events, captions or quotations marked ◆ have extra information provided in the pages at the back of the Almanac.

HOW TO USE THIS ALMANAC AS A DIARY
One week a page for easy reference. The inside front cover extends and folds into a triangular construction for desktop use. The inside back cover folds out to use as your current week marker.

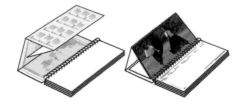

YEAR PLANNER 2022

Day	JANUARY	FEBRUARY	MARCH	APRIL	MAY	JUNE
WED						
THU				WEEK 13		
FRI	WEEK 52			1		
SAT	1			2	WEEK 17	
SUN	2			3	1	
	WEEK 1			WEEK 14	WEEK 18	
MON	3	WEEK 5	WEEK 9	4	2	
TUE	4	1	1	5	3	WEEK 22
WED	5	2	2	6	4	1
THU	6	3	3	7	5	2
FRI	7	4	4	8	6	3
SAT	8	5	5	9	7	4
SUN	9	6	6	10	8	5
	WEEK 2	WEEK 6	WEEK 10	WEEK 15	WEEK 19	WEEK 23
MON	10	7	7	11	9	6
TUE	11	8	8	12	10	7
WED	12	9	9	13	11	8
THU	13	10	10	14	12	9
FRI	14	11	11	15	13	10
SAT	15	12	12	16	14	11
SUN	16	13	13	17	15	12

	WEEK 3	WEEK 7	WEEK 11	WEEK 16	WEEK 20	WEEK 24
MON	17	14	14	18	16	13
TUE	18	15	15	19	17	14
WED	19	16	16	20	18	15
THU	20	17	17	21	19	16
FRI	21	18	18	22	20	17
SAT	22	19	19	23	21	18
SUN	23	20	20	24	22	19
	WEEK 4	WEEK 8	WEEK 12	WEEK 17	WEEK 21	WEEK 25
MON	24	21	21	25	23	20
TUE	25	22	22	26	24	21
WED	26	23	23	27	25	22
THU	27	24	24	28	26	23
FRI	28	25	25	29	27	24
SAT	29	26	26	30	28	25
SUN	30	27	27		29	26
	WEEK 5	WEEK 9	WEEK 13		WEEK 22	WEEK 26
MON	31	28	28		30	27
TUE			29		31	28
WED			30			29
THU			31			30
FRI						
SAT						
SUN						

YEAR PLANNER 2022

	JULY	AUGUST	SEPTEMBER	OCTOBER	NOVEMBER	DECEMBER
WED						WEEK 48
THU	WEEK 26					1
FRI	1			WEEK 39		2
SAT	2			1		3
SUN	3			2		4
	WEEK 27	WEEK 31		WEEK 40		WEEK 49
MON	4	1		3	WEEK 44	5
TUE	5	2		4	1	6
WED	6	3	WEEK 35	5	2	7
THU	7	4	1	6	3	8
FRI	8	5	2	7	4	9
SAT	9	6	3	8	5	10
SUN	10	7	4	9	6	11
	WEEK 28	WEEK 32	WEEK 36	WEEK 41	WEEK 45	WEEK 50
MON	11	8	5	10	7	12
TUE	12	9	6	11	8	13
WED	13	10	7	12	9	14
THU	14	11	8	13	10	15
FRI	15	12	9	14	11	16
SAT	16	13	10	15	12	17
SUN	17	14	11	16	13	18

	WEEK 29	WEEK 33	WEEK 37	WEEK 42	WEEK 46	WEEK 51
MON	18	15	12	17	14	19
TUE	19	16	13	18	15	20
WED	20	17	14	19	16	21
THU	21	18	15	20	17	22
FRI	22	19	16	21	18	23
SAT	23	20	17	22	19	24
SUN	24	21	18	23	20	25

	WEEK 30	WEEK 34	WEEK 38	WEEK 43	WEEK 47	WEEK 52
MON	25	22	19	24	21	26
TUE	26	23	20	25	22	27
WED	27	24	21	26	23	28
THU	28	25	22	27	24	29
FRI	29	26	23	28	25	30
SAT	30	27	24	29	26	31
SUN	31	28	25	30	27	

		WEEK 35	WEEK 39	WEEK 44	WEEK 48	
MON		29	26	31	28	
TUE		30	27		29	
WED		31	28		30	
THU			29			
FRI			30			
SAT						
SUN						

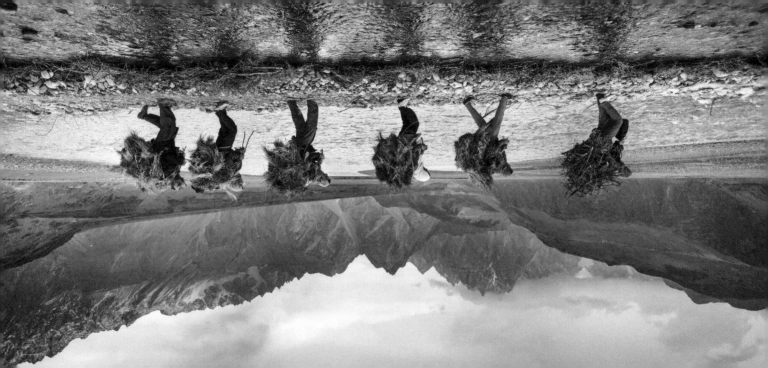

Dwarfed by the mighty Karakoram mountains in Pakistan, a group of Wakhi women from the village of Hunssaini come back from their daily excursion across the Hunza river in search of firewood. ◆

PHOTO: MATTHIEU PALEY/NATIONAL GEOGRAPHIC

27 Monday	28 Tuesday	29 Wednesday	30 Thursday	31 Friday	1 Saturday	2 Sunday
					NEW YEAR'S DAY	

DECEMBER

JANUARY

WEEK 52

None knows the weight of another's burden.
GEORGE HERBERT English poet (1593-1633)

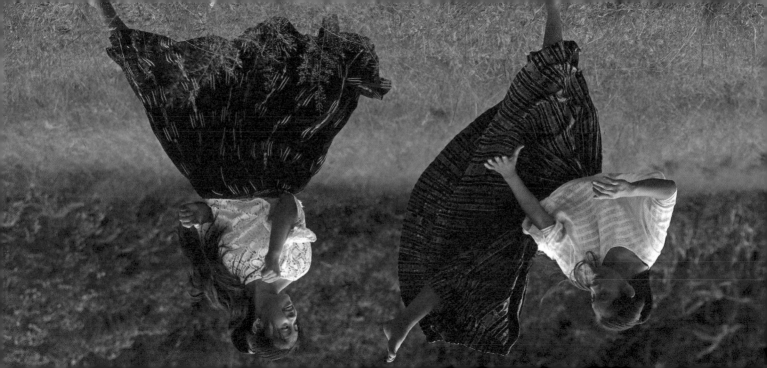

Indigenous Q'eqchi girls practise taekwondo in Tipulcan village, San Pedro Carcha, Guatemala. They take lessons in self-defence to combat the sexist violence and harassment they have suffered in their community.

PHOTO: ESTEBAN BIBA

JANUARY

3 Monday	4 Tuesday	5 Wednesday	6 Thursday	7 Friday	8 Saturday	9 Sunday ☽
PUBLIC HOLIDAY (AUS, CAN, NZ, UK)	PUBLIC HOLIDAY (NZ, SCOT)		EPIPHANY (CHRISTIAN)			

WEEK 1

Never ever accept 'Because You Are A Woman' as a reason for doing or not doing anything.
CHIMAMANDA NGOZI ADICHIE Nigerian writer (1977-)

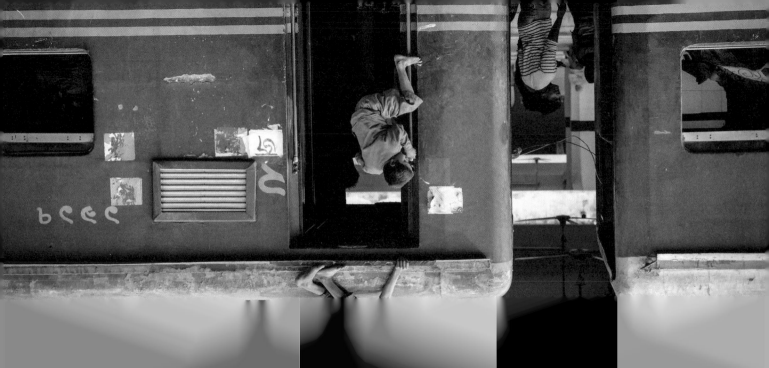

Homeless boys climbing down from the roof as the train pulls into a station. It is estimated that there are as many as 1.5 million children living on the street in Bangladesh, three-quarters of them in Dhaka.

PHOTO: GMB AKASH/PANOS

JANUARY

10 Monday	11 Tuesday	12 Wednesday	13 Thursday	14 Friday	15 Saturday	16 Sunday
			MAGHI (SIKH)			TU B'SHVAT BEGINS (JEWISH)

WEEK 2

Children are living beings – more living than grown-up people who have built shells of habit around themselves.
RABINDRANATH TAGORE Bengali poet (1861-1916)

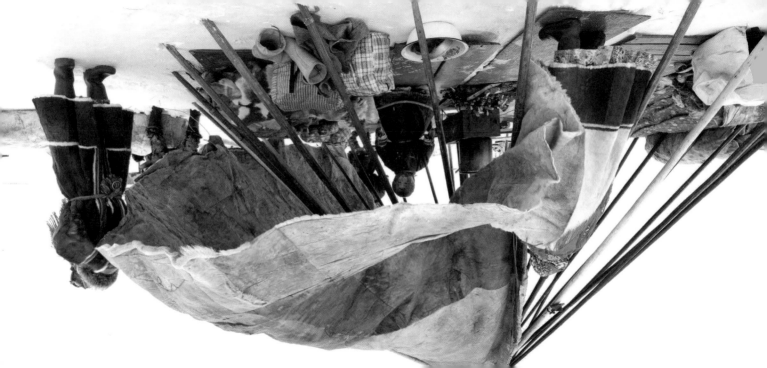

Gosha, a Nenets child, stands inside a part-erected tent or *chum* after the family's arrival at a new campsite in the Yamal Peninsula, Siberia. The Nenets are reindeer herders and the tent is made of reindeer hide.

PHOTO: ELENA CHERNYSHOVA/PANOS

JANUARY

17 Monday ☺
MARTIN LUTHER KING JR
DAY (US)

18 Tuesday

19 Wednesday

20 Thursday

21 Friday

22 Saturday

23 Sunday

WEEK 3

At the end of the day, it isn't where I came from. Maybe home is somewhere I'm going and never have been before.
WARSAN SHIRE British poet (1988-)

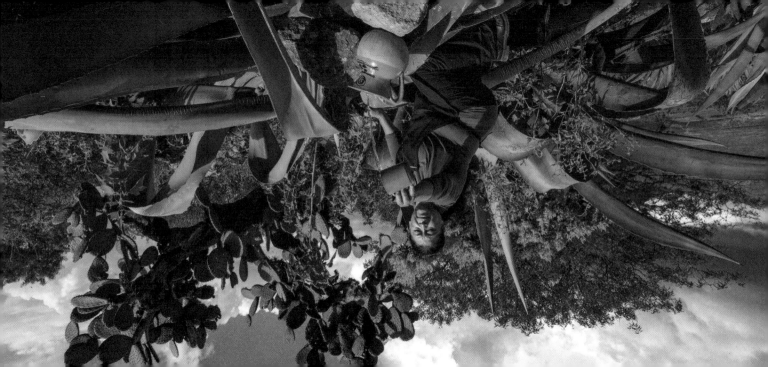

Beatriz and her husband Francisco live in the community of Lagunilla, Mexico, where they produce pulque, a traditional drink extracted from the maguey cactus, once considered to be the beverage of the gods.

24 Monday	25 Tuesday ☾	26 Wednesday	27 Thursday	28 Friday	29 Saturday	30 Sunday
		AUSTRALIA DAY				

JANUARY

WEEK 4

Mineral cactai, quicksilver lizards in the adobe walls... impalpable epiphanies of wind.
OCTAVIO PAZ Mexican poet (1914-98)

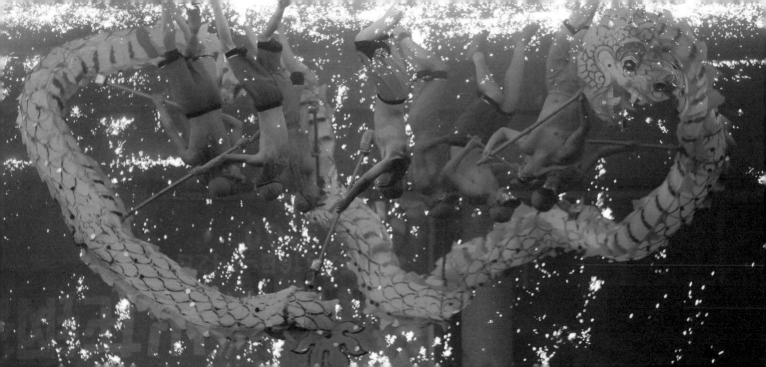

Folk artists perform a fire-dragon dance, part of a traditional performance to celebrate Chinese New Year in the Happy Valley amusement park, Beijing. The sparks they are showered by come from molten iron. ◆

PHOTO: JASON LEE / REUTERS

31 Monday	1 Tuesday ●	2 Wednesday	3 Thursday	4 Friday	5 Saturday	6 Sunday
	CHINESE NEW YEAR	IMBOLC (WICCA)	SETSUBUN-SAI (SHINTO)		VASANT PANCHAMI (HINDU)	WAITANGI DAY (NZ)

JANUARY

FEBRUARY

WEEK 5

We shall go wild with fireworks... And they will plunge into the sky and shatter the darkness.
NATSUKI TAKAYA Japanese manga artist (1973-)

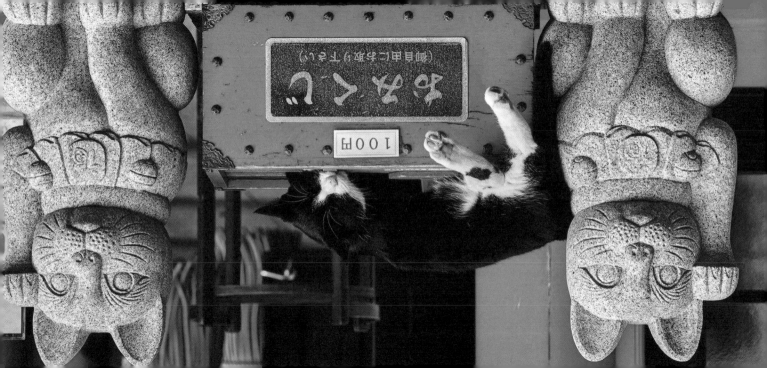

A living cat takes a nap protected by two cat statues in the Gotokuji Temple. This Buddhist shrine in Tokyo, Japan, is said to be the birthplace of the *mankei-neko* cat figurine, which is popular the world over.

PHOTO: TUUL & BRUNO MORANDI

FEBRUARY

7 Monday	8 Tuesday ☽	9 Wednesday	10 Thursday	11 Friday	12 Saturday	13 Sunday
PUBLIC HOLIDAY (NZ)						

WEEK 6

There are two means of refuge from the misery of life – music and cats.
ALBERT SCHWEITZER Alsatian philosopher (1875-1965)

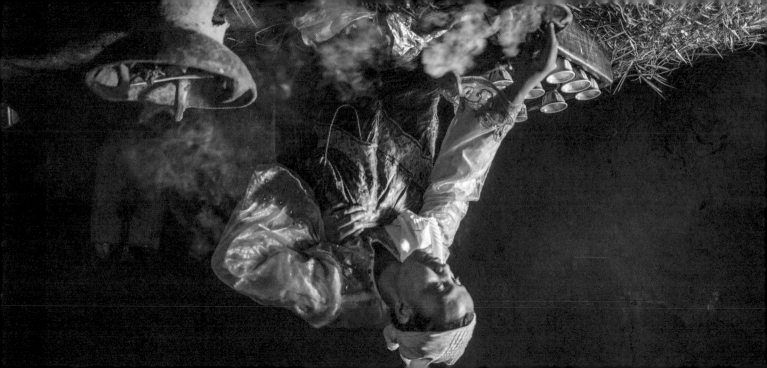

Ramla Sharif roasts coffee inside her home in the village of Choche, Ethiopia. Legend has it Ethiopia is the birthplace of coffee; it is home to more genetic diversity in coffee than the rest of the world combined.

FEBRUARY

14 Monday	15 Tuesday	16 Wednesday ☺	17 Thursday	18 Friday	19 Saturday	20 Sunday
VALENTINE'S DAY	NIRVANA DAY (BUDDHIST)					

WEEK 7

Coffee and love taste best when hot.
ETHIOPIAN PROVERB

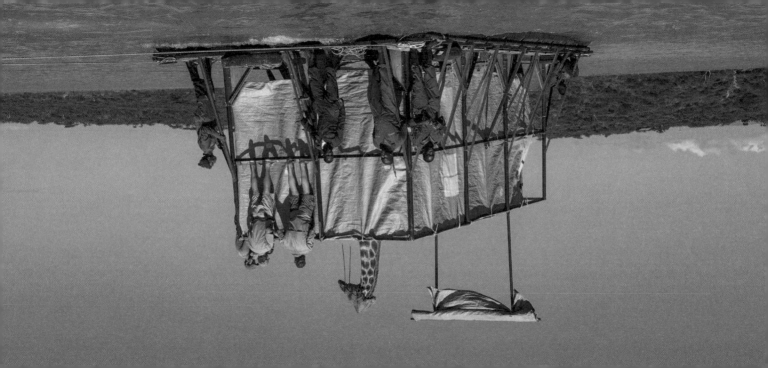

Asiwa, one of eight Nubian giraffes that have been stranded by rising water levels on Longicharo Island in Kenya's Lake Baringo, is rescued on a barge by conservation organizations in December 2020.

FEBRUARY

21 Monday	22 Tuesday	23 Wednesday ☾	24 Thursday	25 Friday	26 Saturday	27 Sunday
PRESIDENTS' DAY (US)						

WEEK 8

If I know a song of Africa, of the giraffe and the African new moon lying on her back, of the ploughs in the fields
and the sweaty faces of the coffee pickers, does Africa know a song of me?
ISAK DINESEN/KAREN BLIXEN Danish author (1885-1962)

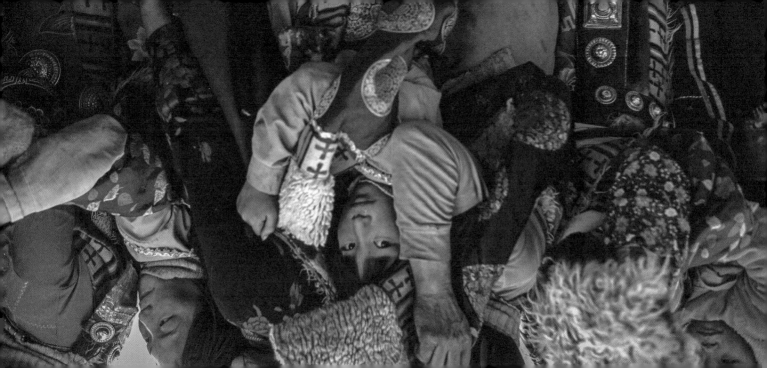

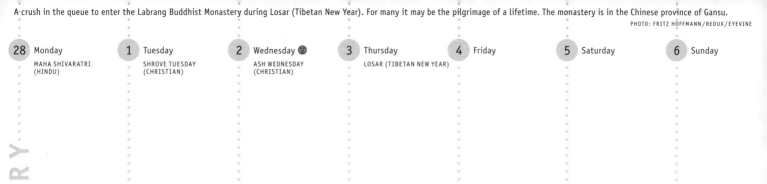

A crush in the queue to enter the Labrang Buddhist Monastery during Losar (Tibetan New Year). For many it may be the pilgrimage of a lifetime. The monastery is in the Chinese province of Gansu.

28 Monday	1 Tuesday	2 Wednesday	3 Thursday	4 Friday	5 Saturday	6 Sunday
MAHA SHIVARATRI (HINDU)	SHROVE TUESDAY (CHRISTIAN)	ASH WEDNESDAY (CHRISTIAN)	LOSAR (TIBETAN NEW YEAR)			

FEBRUARY

MARCH

WEEK 9

Choose to be optimistic, it feels better.
THE DALAI LAMA Tibetan Buddhist spiritual leader (1935-)

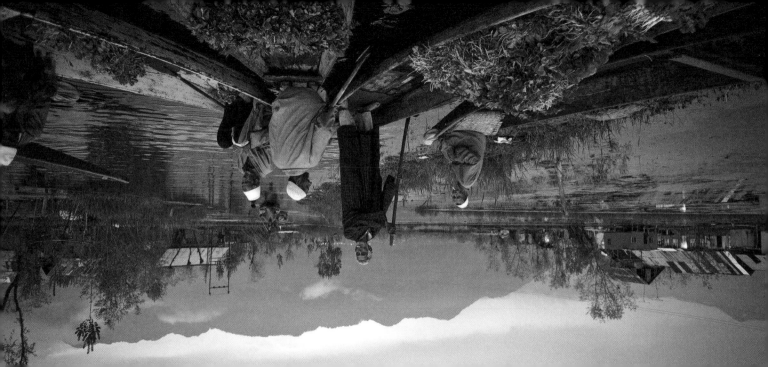

Kashmiri men sell their vegetables at a floating market on the picturesque Dal Lake in the summer capital of Srinagar in the Indian-held state of Kashmir, more frequented now by soldiers than by tourists.

PHOTO: AMI VITALE

7 Monday	8 Tuesday	9 Wednesday	10 Thursday ☽	11 Friday	12 Saturday	13 Sunday
	INTERNATIONAL WOMEN'S DAY					CLOCKS CHANGE (CAN/US)

MARCH

WEEK 10

Srinagar is a medieval city dying in a modern war... Srinagar is never winning and never being defeated.
BASHARAT PEER Kashmiri-American journalist and author (1977-)

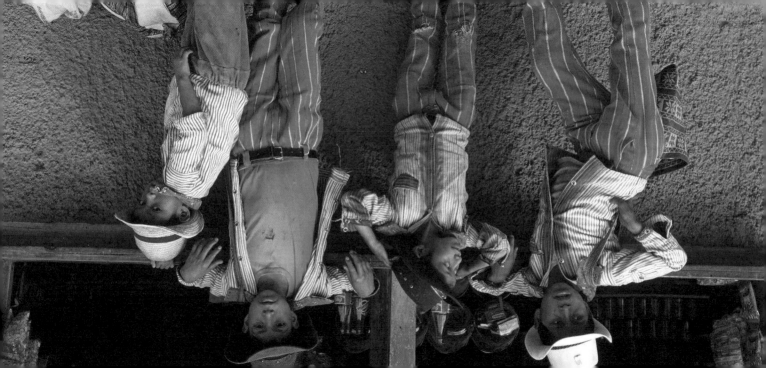

Aiming for the quintessence of cool. Boys in the village of Todos Santos de Cuchumatan in Guatemala show a level of awareness of the camera worthy of iconic movie star James Dean.

PHOTO: TUUL & BRUNO MORANDI

14 Monday	15 Tuesday	16 Wednesday	17 Thursday	18 Friday ☺	19 Saturday	20 Sunday
		PURIM BEGINS (JEWISH)	ST PATRICK'S DAY (IRE)	HOLI (HINDU), HOLA MAHALLA (SIKH)		EQUINOX

MARCH

WEEK 11

To be natural is such a very difficult pose to keep up.
OSCAR WILDE, British dramatist and wit (1854-1900)

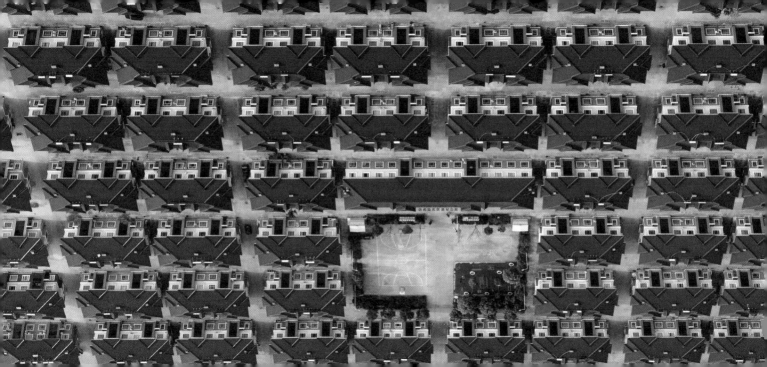

Rows of identical houses with a communal yard or garden in the middle, seen from above the city of Jiangyin, which is situated on the Yangtze River near Changzhou, China.

21 Monday	22 Tuesday	23 Wednesday	24 Thursday	25 Friday ☾	26 Saturday	27 Sunday
						CLOCKS CHANGE (EUROPE)

MARCH

WEEK 12

When you increase the number of gardens, you increase the number of heavens too!
MEHMET MURAT İLDAN Turkish writer (1965-)

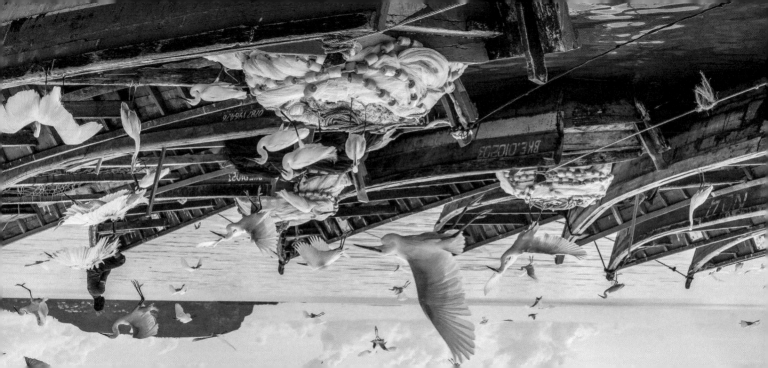

White egrets flock around fishing boats in Bukoba, Tanzania, after a night of storms on Lake Victoria. The main fish caught here are 'dagaa' or silver cyprinids. In the background is the island of Musira.

28 Monday	29 Tuesday	30 Wednesday	31 Thursday	1 Friday ●	2 Saturday	3 Sunday
					RAMADAN BEGINS (MUSLIM)	CLOCKS CHANGE (AUS/NZ)

MARCH

APRIL

WEEK 13

Kila ndege huruka na mbawa zake Every bird flies with its own wings.
KISWAHILI PROVERB

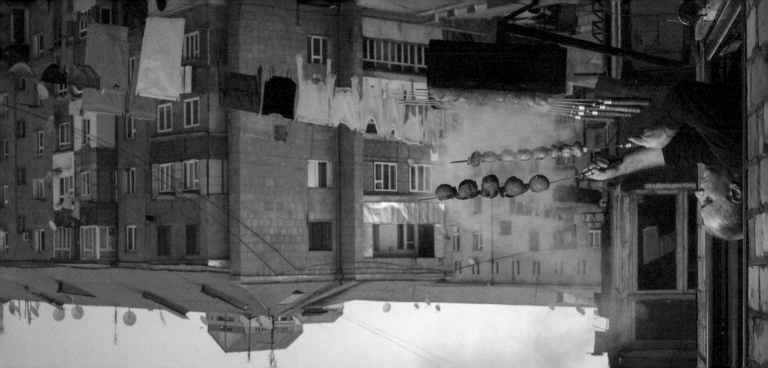

David Abgaryan cooks dinner on his barbecue, which is suspended outside the window of his fourth-floor apartment in Stepanakert, Nagorno-Karabakh – the territory disputed between Armenia and Azerbaijan. ◆

4 Monday

5 Tuesday

6 Wednesday

7 Thursday
WORLD HEALTH DAY

8 Friday

9 Saturday ☽

10 Sunday
PALM SUNDAY
(CHRISTIAN)

APRIL

WEEK 14

Ask not what you can do for your country. Ask what's for lunch.
ORSON WELLES US filmmaker (1915-85)

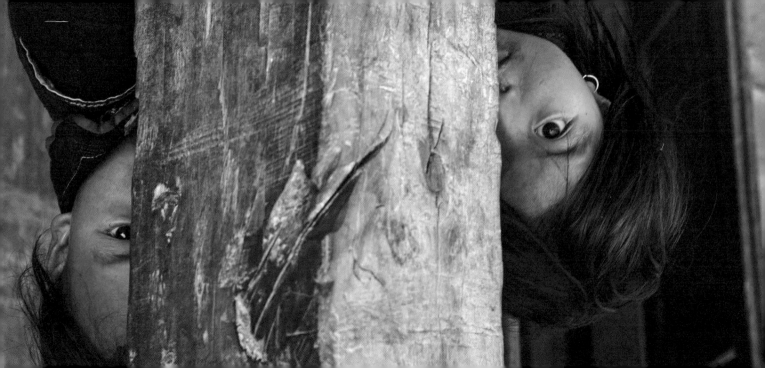

Peek-a-boo. Schoolgirls from the Black Hmong ethnic group play hide and seek with the photographer. The Hmong live in the hill country near Sa Pa in northern Vietnam.

PHOTO: TUUL & BRUNO MORANDI

11 Monday

12 Tuesday

13 Wednesday

14 Thursday
BAISAKHI
(SIKH NEW YEAR)

15 Friday
GOOD FRIDAY (CHRISTIAN),
PASSOVER BEGINS (JEWISH)

16 Saturday ☺

17 Sunday
EASTER DAY
(CHRISTIAN)

APRIL

WEEK 15

Now let us play hide and seek. Should you hide in my heart it would not be difficult to find you.
But should you hide behind your own shell, then it would be useless for anyone to seek you.
KHALIL GIBRAN Lebanese-American writer (1883-1931)

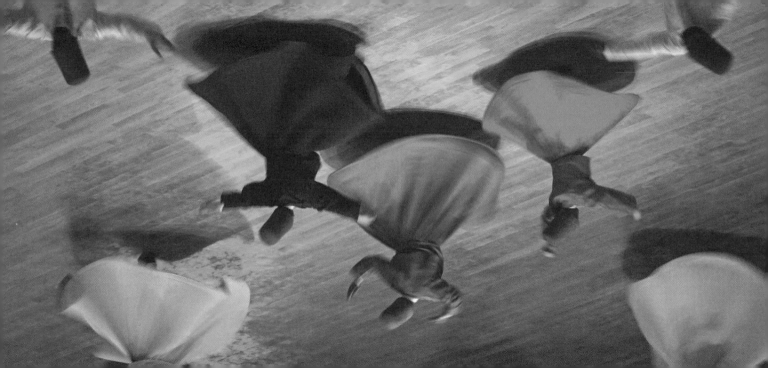

Sema dancers in Konya, Turkey. Sema means 'hearing' and refers to some of the ceremonies in Sufism that involve prayer, song and dance. It was dancing like this that Europeans described as 'whirling dervishes'.

PHOTO: TUUL & BRUNO MORANDI

APRIL

18 Monday	19 Tuesday	20 Wednesday	21 Thursday	22 Friday	23 Saturday ☾	24 Sunday
PUBLIC HOLIDAY (AUS, CAN, NZ, UK EXCEPT SCOT)						

WEEK 16

Stop acting so small. You are the universe in ecstatic motion.
RUMI Persian poet and Sufi mystic, who was buried in Konya (1207-73)

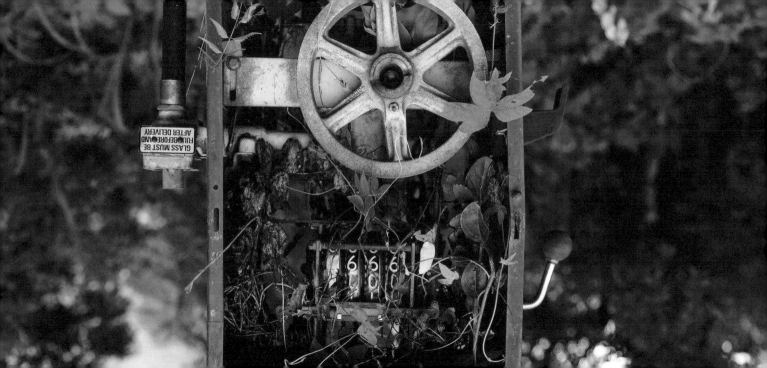

GLASS MUST BE
FULL BEFORE AND
AFTER DELIVERY

Nature can reclaim anything, given time, as proven by this old petrol pump near the decommissioned train station in Voi, Kenya, which lies between Tsavo West national park and the coastal city of Mombasa.

25 Monday
ANZAC DAY (AUS/NZ)

26 Tuesday

27 Wednesday
YOM HASHOAH BEGINS
(JEWISH)

28 Thursday

29 Friday

30 Saturday

1 Sunday
INTERNATIONAL
WORKERS' DAY,
BEALTAINE (PAGAN)

APRIL

MAY

WEEK 17

The power of nature can make fun of the power of man at any time.
MEHMET MURAT İLDAN Turkish writer (1965-)

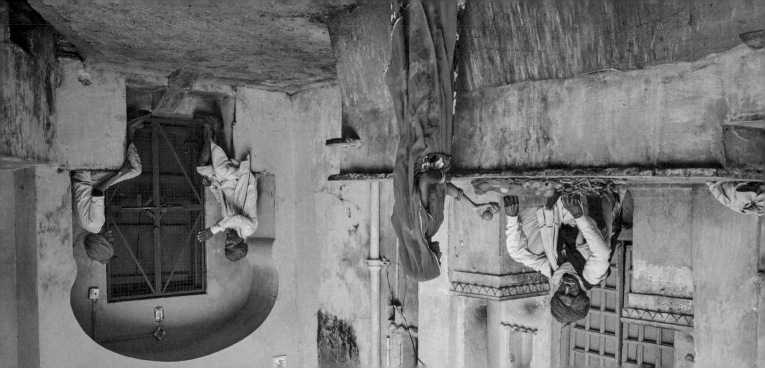

In a narrow street of the 'blue city' – Jodhpur, in the Indian state of Rajasthan – a man sells his vegetables. Only the buildings in the old town at the foot of the Mehrangarh fortress have this unique colouring. ◆

PHOTO: TUUL & BRUNO MORANDI

2 Monday	3 Tuesday	4 Wednesday	5 Thursday	6 Friday	7 Saturday	8 Sunday
EID AL FITR (MUSLIM), PUBLIC HOLIDAY (UK)						

MAY

WEEK 18

Let me, O let me bathe my soul in colours; let me swallow the sunset and drink the rainbow.
KHALIL GIBRAN Lebanese-American writer (1883-1931)

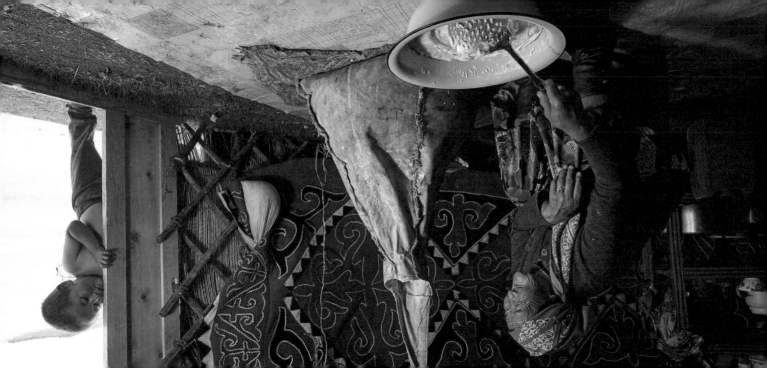

Dinka, a Kazakh child in Bayan-Ölgii Province in western Mongolia, is waiting impatiently to taste the delicious cream that his grandmother Bejei has just been churning inside the sheepskin bag.

PHOTO: ALESSANDRA MENICONZI

9 Monday ☽	10 Tuesday	11 Wednesday	12 Thursday	13 Friday	14 Saturday	15 Sunday

MAY

WEEK 19

The supreme treasure is knowledge, the middle treasure is children, and the lowest treasure is material wealth.
MONGOLIAN PROVERB

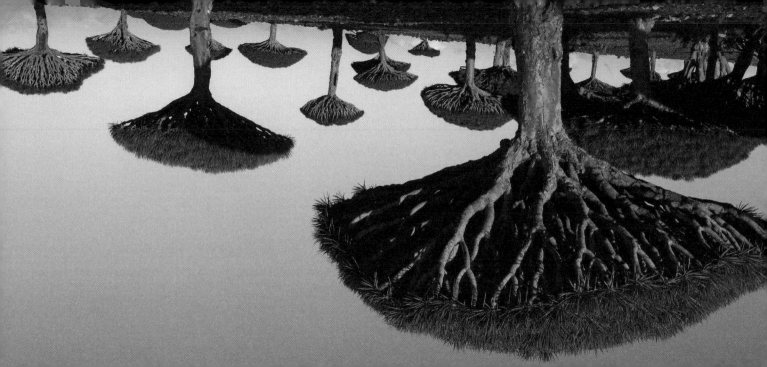

These dragon blood trees (*Dracaena cinnabari*), with their umbrella-shaped crowns, are unique to the Socotra archipelago in the Arabian Sea, which belongs to Yemen. They are named after their dark-red resin.

16 Monday ☺	17 Tuesday	18 Wednesday	19 Thursday	20 Friday	21 Saturday	22 Sunday ☾

MAY

WEEK 20

He who wants everything gets nothing.
YEMENI PROVERB

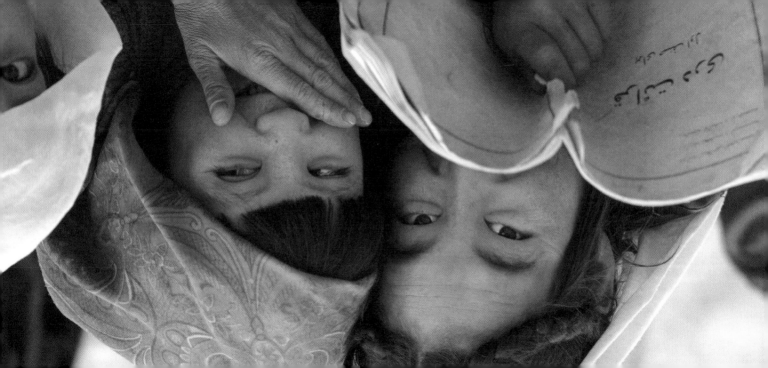

Girls learning to read in a school that was rebuilt in the village of Anbar Somuch when more than 100 families returned home following the fall of the repressive Taliban regime in Afghanistan in 2001.

PHOTO: AMI VITALE

23 Monday	24 Tuesday	25 Wednesday	26 Thursday	27 Friday	28 Saturday	29 Sunday
VICTORIA DAY (CAN)			ASCENSION DAY (CHRISTIAN)	VISAKHA PUJA (BUDDHIST)		ASCENSION OF THE BAHA'U'LLAH (BAHA'I)

MAY

WEEK 21

To the women of my beloved country: believe in yourselves. You are strong. Speak up about your dreams and your goals every day so that everyone knows that you exist and you have the right to choose.
SONITA ALIZADEH Afghan rapper and activist (1996-)

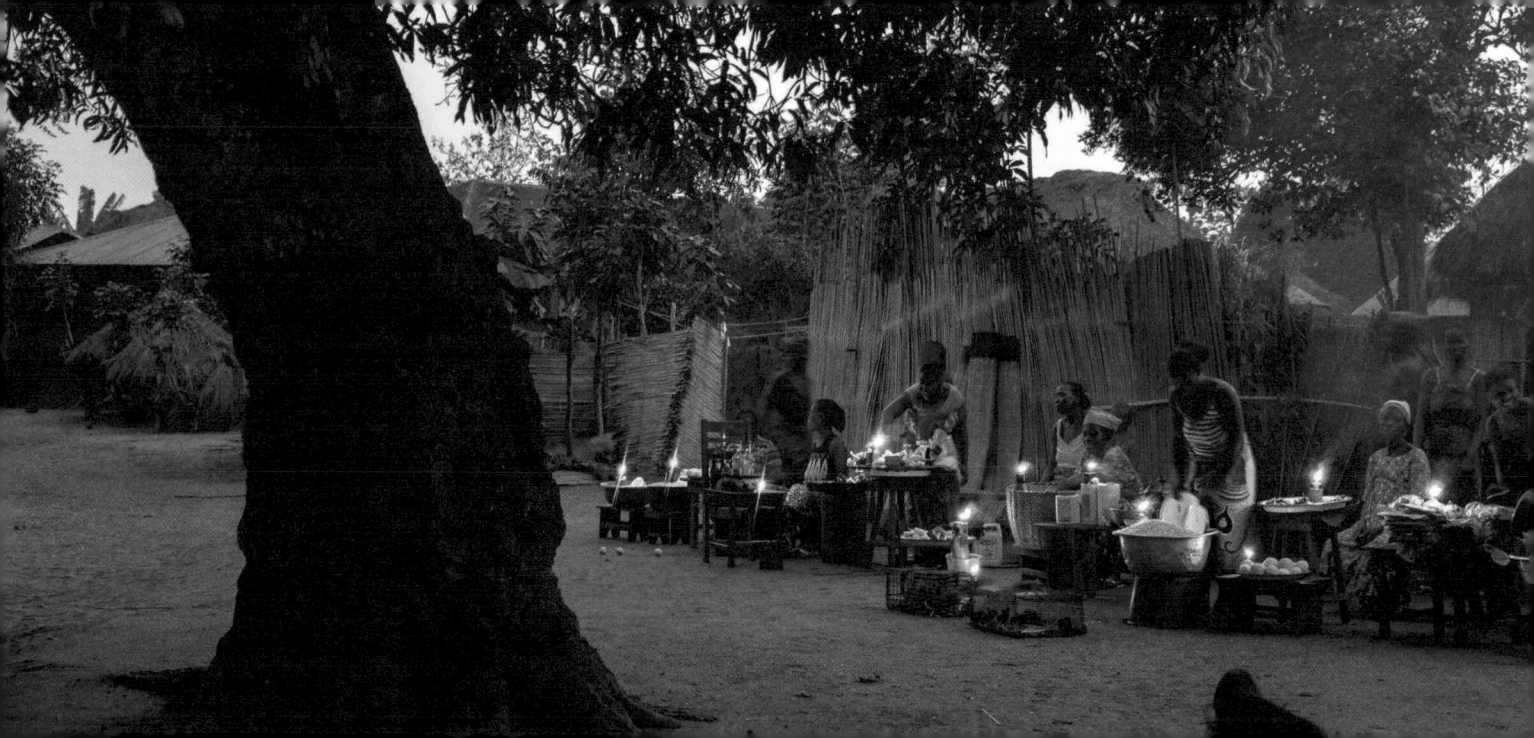

This market, illuminated only by candlelight and kerosene lamps, takes place each night beneath a palaver tree in Kokahoue, Benin. Kokahoue is one of nine nearby villages that are off the electricity grid.

30 Monday ◉
MEMORIAL DAY (US)

31 Tuesday

1 Wednesday

2 Thursday
PUBLIC HOLIDAY (UK)

3 Friday
QUEEN'S PLATINUM JUBILEE,
PUBLIC HOLIDAY (UK)

4 Saturday
SHAVUOT BEGINS (JEWISH)

5 Sunday
WORLD ENVIRONMENT DAY,
PENTECOST (CHRISTIAN)

MAY

JUNE

WEEK 22

We can only speak the truth when we turn off the light.
BENINESE PROVERB

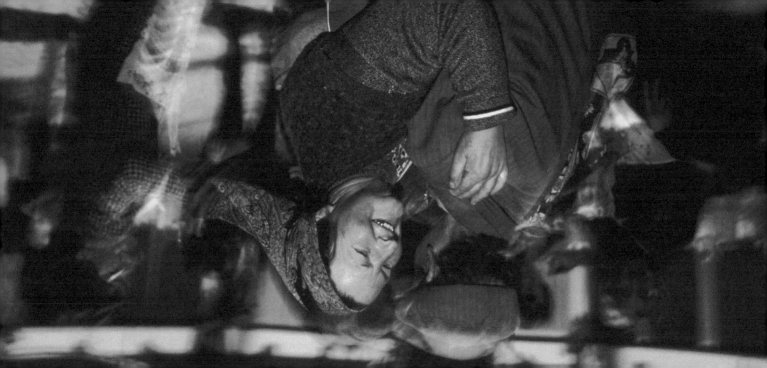

Lost in music. The ecstasy of dance is by no means the exclusive province of the young, as this couple at a wedding celebration demonstrate. The wedding is in the ethnic Ukrainian village of Crisan in Romania.

PHOTO: ED KASHI/VII/REDUX/EYEVINE

6 Monday	7 Tuesday ☽	8 Wednesday	9 Thursday	10 Friday	11 Saturday	12 Sunday
QUEEN'S BIRTHDAY (NZ)						

JUNE

WEEK 23

Our biological rhythms are the symphony of the cosmos, music embedded deep within us to which we dance, even when we can't name the tune.
DEEPAK CHOPRA Indian-American author (1946-)

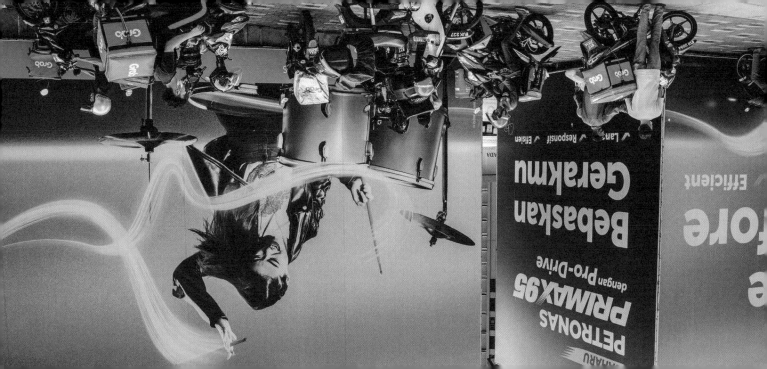

Couriers and food deliverers wait on their motor scooters for jobs beside a huge advertisement for Petronas Primax 95 fuel. They are around the corner from the Petronas Twin Towers in Kuala Lumpur, Malaysia.

13 Monday
QUEEN'S BIRTHDAY (AUS)

14 Tuesday ☺

15 Wednesday

16 Thursday

17 Friday

18 Saturday

19 Sunday

JUNE

WEEK 24

Rock'n'roll might not solve your problems, but it does let you dance all over them.
PETE TOWNSHEND British musician (1945-)

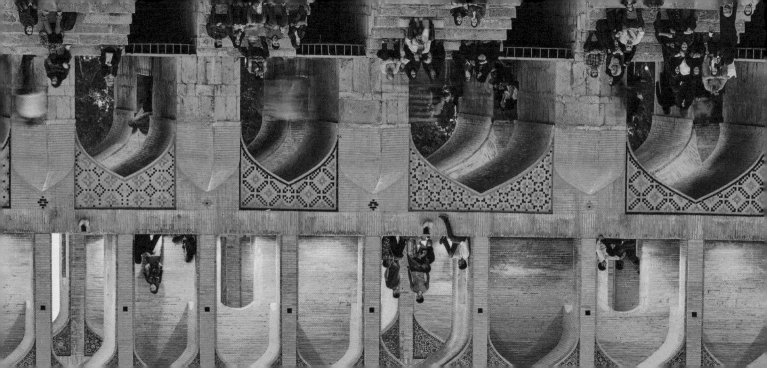

Golden light illuminates the Khaju Bridge over the River Zayandeh in ancient Isfahan – a popular evening meeting place for locals. Once the Persian capital, Isfahan is now Iran's third-largest city.

20 Monday
WORLD REFUGEE DAY

21 Tuesday ☾
SOLSTICE

22 Wednesday

23 Thursday

24 Friday

25 Saturday

26 Sunday

JUNE

WEEK 25

This universe is not outside of you. Look inside yourself; everything that you want, you are already that.
RUMI Persian poet (1207-73)

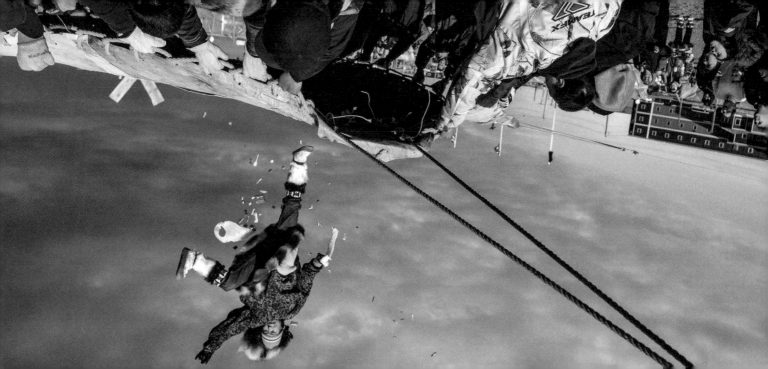

An Inupiat woman jumping on a trampoline made of walrus skin during Nalukataq, an annual festival held at the end of June in Barrow, Alaska, to celebrate the success of the whale-hunting season.

PHOTO: VLAD SOKHIN/PANOS

27 Monday	28 Tuesday	29 Wednesday ●	30 Thursday	1 Friday	2 Saturday	3 Sunday
				CANADA DAY		

JUNE

JULY

WEEK 26

Mama exhorted her children at every opportunity to 'jump at the sun'. We might not land on the sun, but at least we would get off the ground.
ZORA NEALE HURSTON US author (1891-1960)

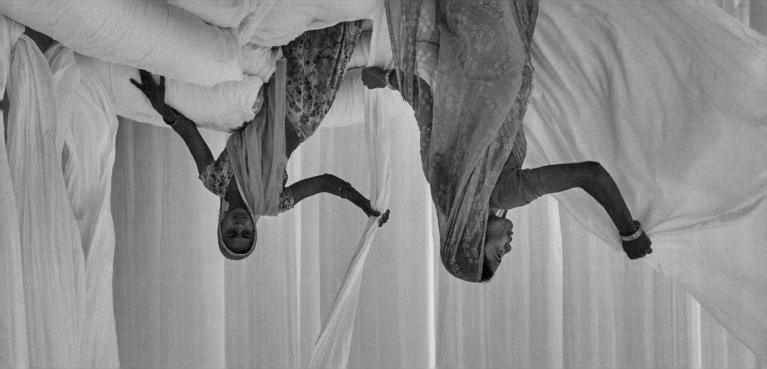

Wafting in a gentle breeze: textiles hung up for air drying are monitored and gathered by women working in a sari factory located in the northwestern state of Rajasthan, India.

4 Monday	5 Tuesday	6 Wednesday	7 Thursday ☽	8 Friday	9 Saturday	10 Sunday
INDEPENDENCE DAY (US)					EID AL ADHA BEGINS (MUSLIM)	

JULY

WEEK 27

The sari's radiance, vigour and variety, produced by a single straight length of cloth, should give us in the West pause and make us think twice about the zipper, the dart and the shoulder pad.
NAVEEN PATNAIK Indian politician (1946-)

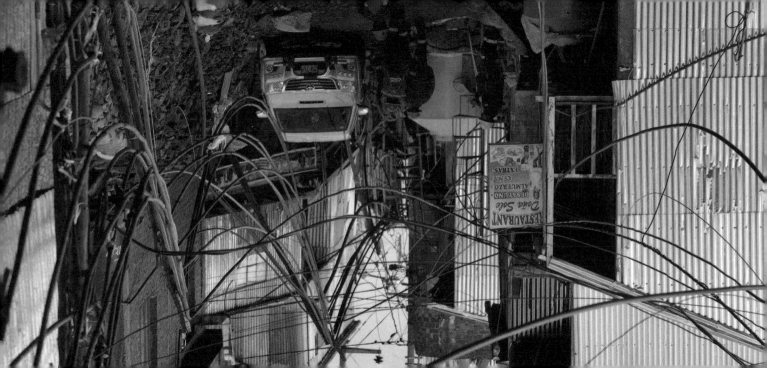

A chaotic profusion of electricity cables hangs above a street in La Rinconada in Peru. This gold-mining town is, at more than 5,200 metres, the highest permanently settled community in the world.

PHOTO: PASCAL MAITRE/PANOS

11 Monday	12 Tuesday	13 Wednesday ☺	14 Thursday	15 Friday	16 Saturday	17 Sunday
		OBON (SHINTO)				

JULY

WEEK 28

We will make electricity so cheap that only the rich will burn candles.
THOMAS ALVA EDISON US inventor (1847-1931)

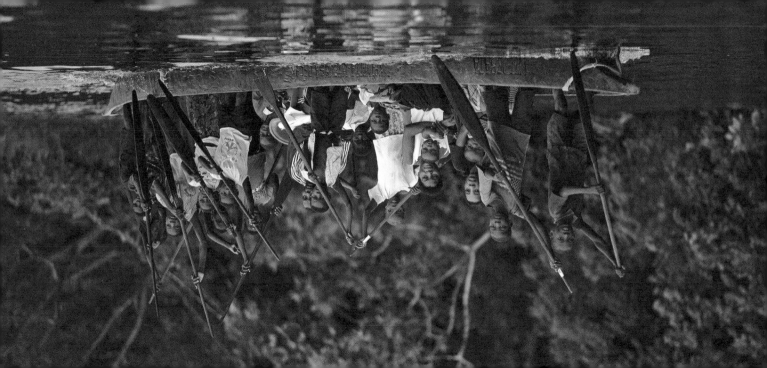

Standing room only. A family with 18 children makes its way to church on a Sunday by pirogue on the River Congo. The family lives between the towns of Lisala and Mobeka in the Democratic Republic of Congo.

PHOTO: PASCAL MAITRE/PANOS

18 Monday	19 Tuesday	20 Wednesday ☾	21 Thursday	22 Friday	23 Saturday	24 Sunday

JULY

WEEK 29

No matter how full the river, it still wants to grow.
CONGOLESE PROVERB

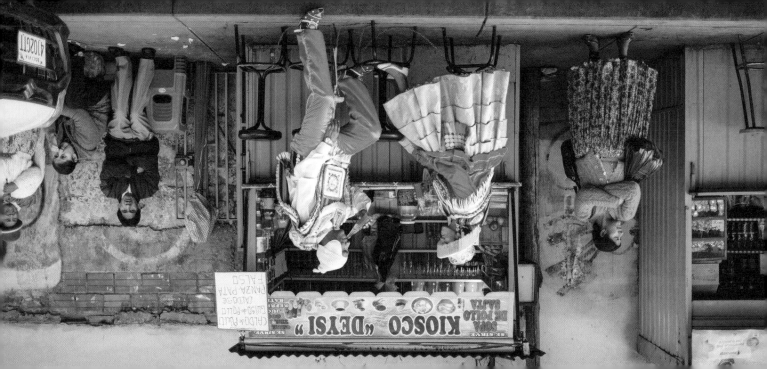

Wilma Canchi and Raul Limachi take a well-earned break from their dancing at a folk festival in the Bolivian capital, La Paz. Their Kullawada dance – popular with the Aymara people – dates back to Inca times. ◆

25 Monday

26 Tuesday

27 Wednesday

28 Thursday ☻

29 Friday
MUSLIM NEW YEAR

30 Saturday

31 Sunday

JULY

WEEK 30

If you marry wise judgement, peace will become your brother-in-law.
BOLIVIAN PROVERB

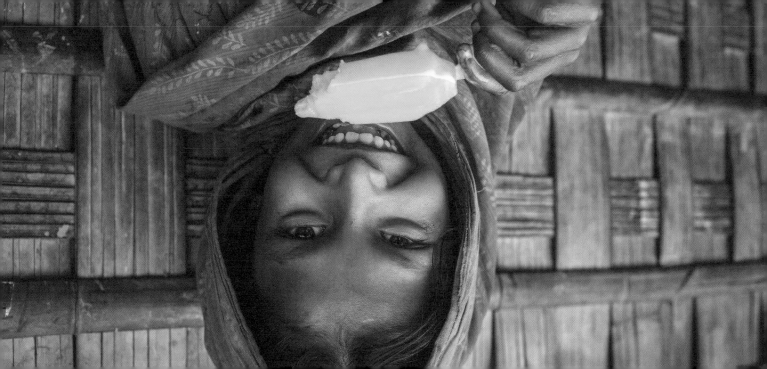

Ten-year-old Shima samples an ice lolly amid the perpetually hot weather in the Bangladeshi capital, Dhaka. She takes care of her younger brother while her mother goes to work in a textile factory.

1 Monday	2 Tuesday	3 Wednesday	4 Thursday	5 Friday ☽	6 Saturday	7 Sunday
PUBLIC HOLIDAY (SCOT)						ASHURA (MUSLIM)

AUGUST

WEEK 31

There were some problems only coffee and ice cream could fix.
AMAL EL-MOHTAR Canadian poet (1984-)

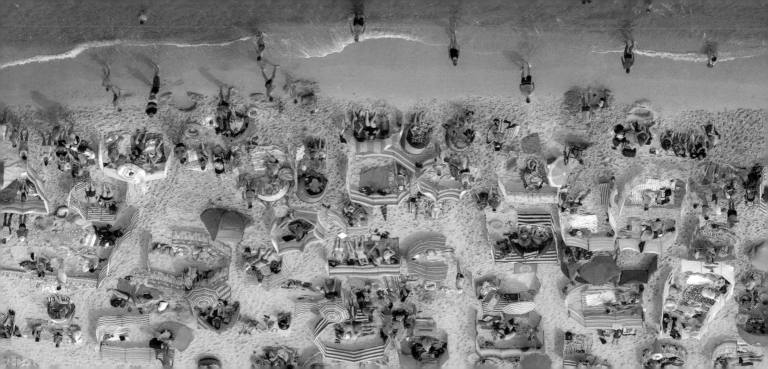

Crowds have flocked to this public beach in Wladyslawowo, on Poland's Baltic coast, during the sunny first weekend of August 2020. Despite the Covid-19 pandemic, social distancing is little in evidence.

8 Monday	**9** Tuesday	**10** Wednesday	**11** Thursday	**12** Friday ☺	**13** Saturday	**14** Sunday
				INTERNATIONAL YOUTH DAY		

AUGUST

WEEK 32

Because there's nothing more beautiful than the way the ocean refuses to stop kissing the shoreline, no matter how many times it's sent away.
SARAH KAY US poet (1988-)

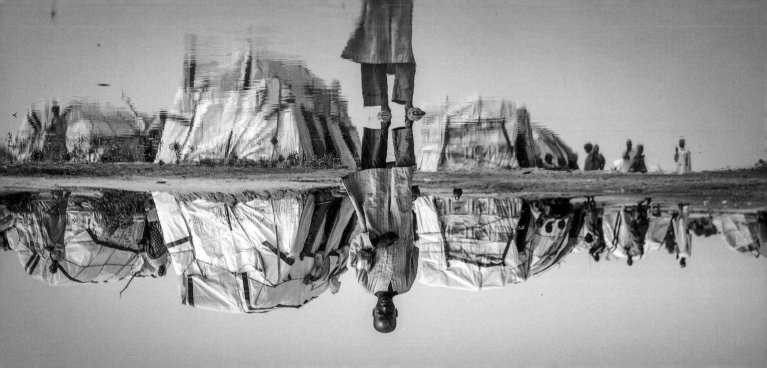

A child walks through a puddle in Muna Garage, an IDP camp on the outskirts of Maiduguri, in northern Nigeria, where an estimated 50,000 people have taken refuge after fleeing Boko Haram.

15 Monday	**16** Tuesday	**17** Wednesday	**18** Thursday	**19** Friday ☾	**20** Saturday	**21** Sunday

AUGUST

WEEK 33

A person who has children does not die.
NIGERIAN PROVERB

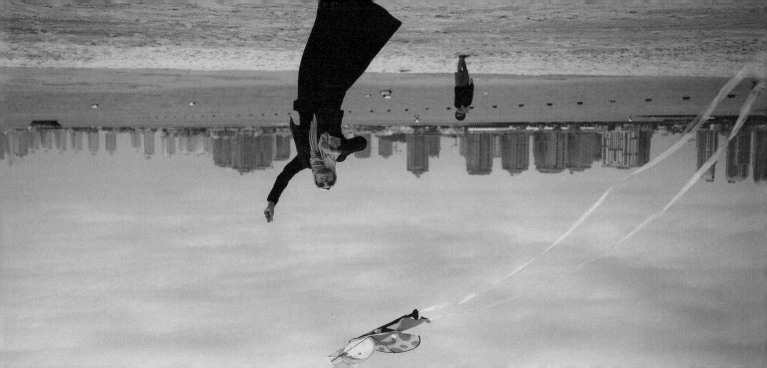

Flying a kite at Katara Beach, a 1.5-kilometre-long stretch of sand in Doha, the capital of Qatar – a popular place for watersports. Women cannot swim here unless their bodies are completely covered.

PHOTO: CORINNA KERN/REUTERS

22 Monday	23 Tuesday	24 Wednesday	25 Thursday	26 Friday	27 Saturday ●	28 Sunday
	PARYUSHANA PARVARAMBHA (JAIN)					

AUGUST

WEEK 34

Throw your dreams into space like a kite, and you do not know what it will bring back, a new life, a new friend, a new love, a new country.
ANAIS NIN Cuban-French-American writer (1903-77)

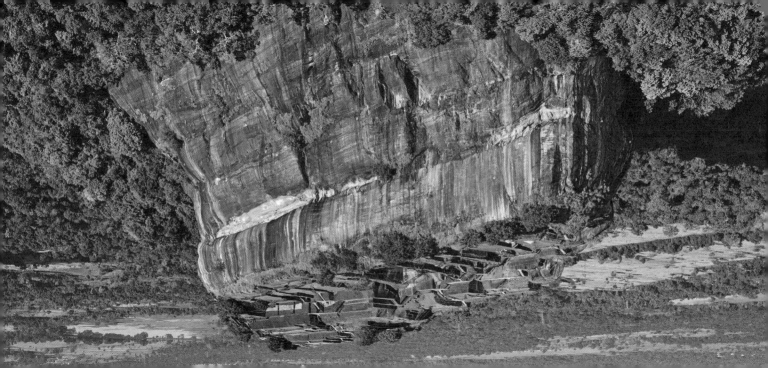

Impregnable altitude: the Sigiriya fortress near Dambulla in Sri Lanka is a UNESCO World Heritage site. According to ancient chronicles, King Kashyapa (477-495) selected this spot to build his palace.

29 Monday
PUBLIC HOLIDAY
(UK EXCEPT SCOT)

30 Tuesday

31 Wednesday

1 Thursday

2 Friday

3 Saturday ☽

4 Sunday

AUGUST

SEPTEMBER

WEEK 35

The proper way to understand any social system was to view it from above.
ELEANOR CATTON New Zealand/Aotearoa writer (1985-)

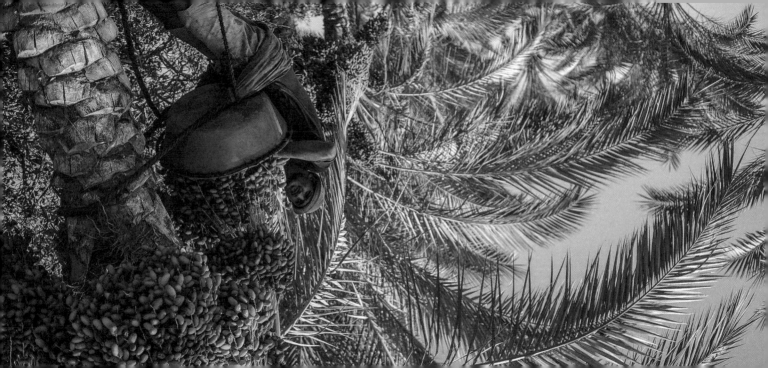

Climbing high, a man picks red dates from palm trees in Deir al Balah town in the central section of the Gaza Strip, part of the Occupied Palestinian Territories. Gaza has around 150,000 date-producing palms.

SEPTEMBER

5 Monday	6 Tuesday	7 Wednesday	8 Thursday	9 Friday	10 Saturday ☺	11 Sunday
LABOUR DAY (CAN), LABOR DAY (US)						

WEEK 36

The roots of the aged palm tree exceed those of the young one; the old have a greater attachment to the world.

SAIB TABRIZI Persian poet (1592-1676)

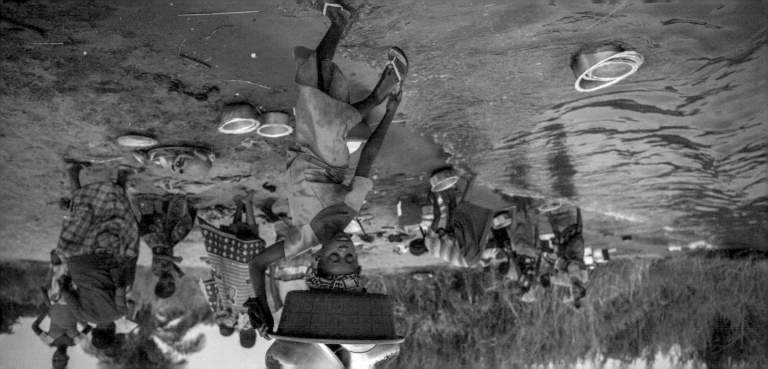

Girls from the village of Nkongwa, Tanzania, washing pots on the shores of Lake Tanganyika. The community is dependent on the lake for its drinking water as well as for washing.

12 Monday	**13** Tuesday	**14** Wednesday	**15** Thursday	**16** Friday	**17** Saturday ☾	**18** Sunday

SEPTEMBER

WEEK 37

To measure a country's wealth by its gross national product is to measure things, not satisfactions.
JULIUS NYERERE Tanzanian leader (1922-99)

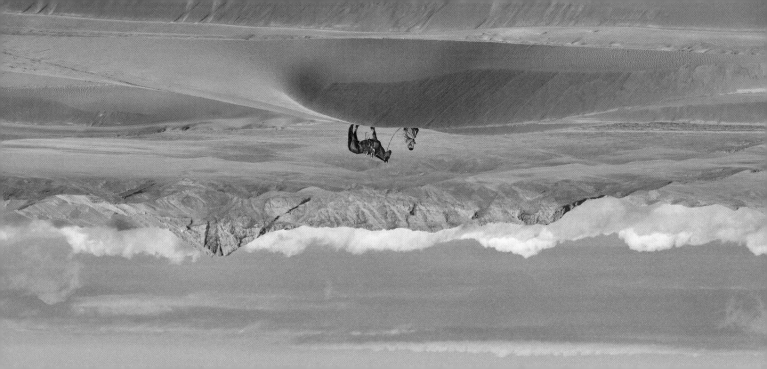

A horse and its rider alone amid the immensity of the desert and the mountains. They are riding through Zavkhan province in the far western reaches of Mongolia.

PHOTO: TUUL & BRUNO MORANDI

SEPTEMBER

WEEK 38

19 Monday	**20** Tuesday	**21** Wednesday	**22** Thursday	**23** Friday	**24** Saturday	**25** Sunday 🌑
			EQUINOX			CLOCKS CHANGE (NZ), ROSH HASHANAH BEGINS (JEWISH)

The distance between heaven and earth is no greater than one thought.
MONGOLIAN PROVERB

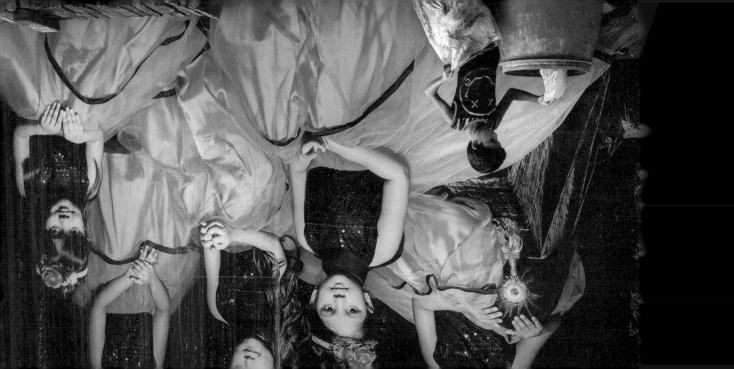

In front of a large billboard in Dhaka, Bangladesh, a boy looks through a rubbish bin for plastics to recycle. Street children collect plastic waste and sell it for as little as 10 taka (11 US cents) a kilogram.

PHOTO: GMB AKASH/PANOS

26 Monday	27 Tuesday	28 Wednesday	29 Thursday	30 Friday	1 Saturday	2 Sunday
NAVARATRI BEGINS (HINDU)						CLOCKS CHANGE (AUS)

SEPTEMBER

OCTOBER

WEEK 39

There can be no keener revelation of a society's soul than the way in which it treats its children.
NELSON MANDELA South African leader (1918-2013)

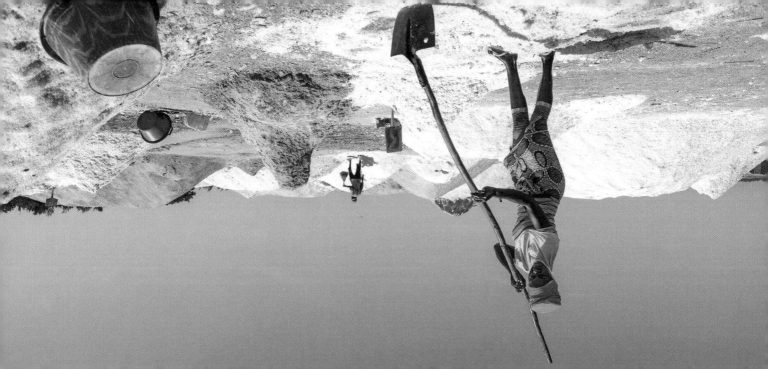

Piling up salt on the shores of Lake Retba in Senegal. While men tend to gather salt from the lake in boats, women have to carry the salt from the boats, for which they are paid less than two dollars a day. ◆

3 Monday ☽

4 Tuesday
YOM KIPPUR BEGINS
(JEWISH)

5 Wednesday

6 Thursday

7 Friday

8 Saturday
MAWLID AL NABI BEGINS
(SUNNI MUSLIM)

9 Sunday ☺
SUKKOT BEGINS
(JEWISH)

OCTOBER

WEEK 40

I shivered in those solitudes when I heard the voice of the salt in the desert.
PABLO NERUDA Chilean poet and diplomat (1904-73)

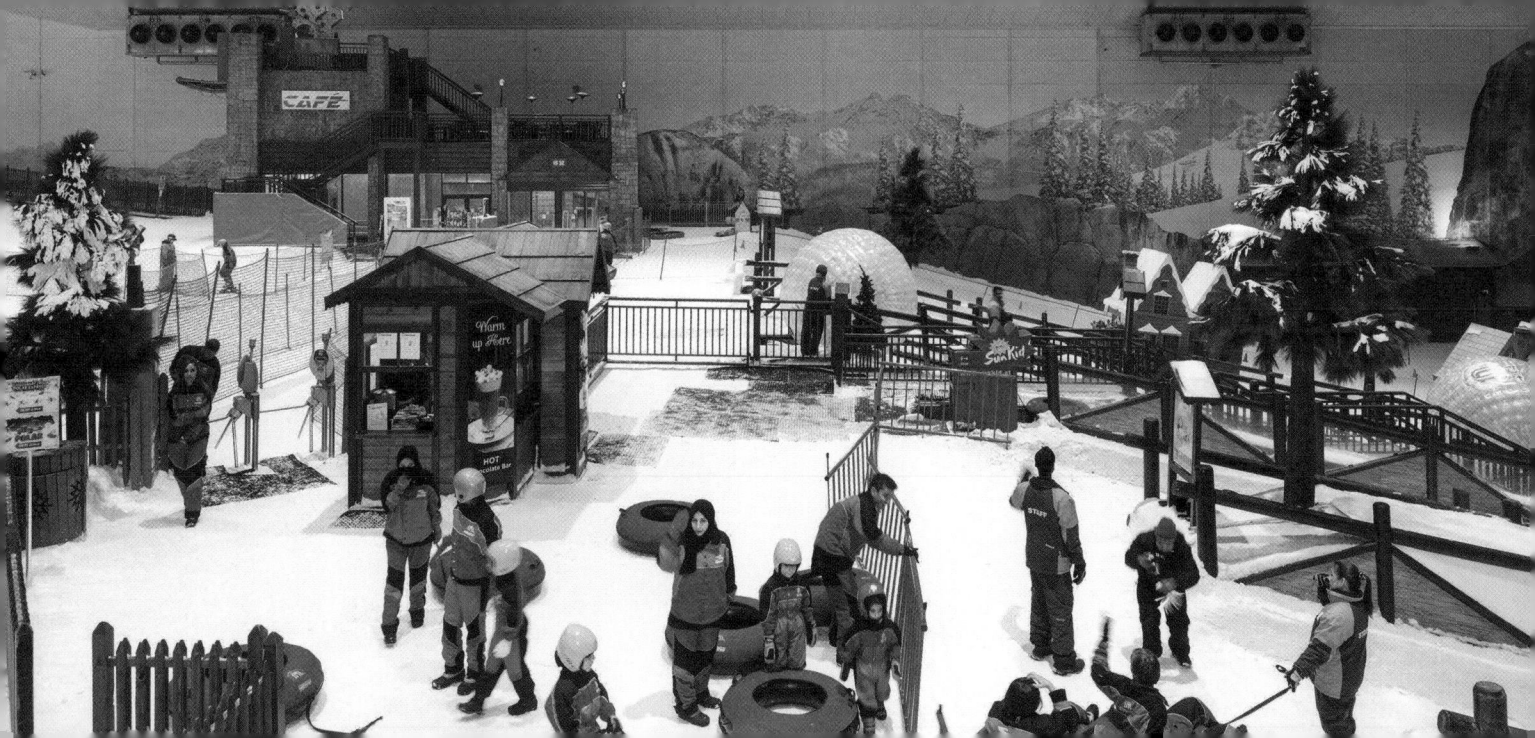

The unsustainable ultimate? Playing on sleds in a 22,500-square-metre indoor ski resort within the Mall of the Emirates – one of the world's largest shopping centres, situated in the desert city of Dubai.

PHOTO: NICK HANNES/PANOS

10 Monday	**11** Tuesday	**12** Wednesday	**13** Thursday	**14** Friday	**15** Saturday	**16** Sunday
INDIGENOUS PEOPLES' DAY (US), THANKSGIVING (CAN)		MAWLID AL NABI BEGINS (SHIA MUSLIM)				WORLD FOOD DAY

OCTOBER

WEEK 41

I like to believe that I have a better understanding of ground realities than those who live in air-conditioned elite areas in Dubai and Karachi.
REHAM KHAN British-Pakistani journalist and filmmaker (1973-)

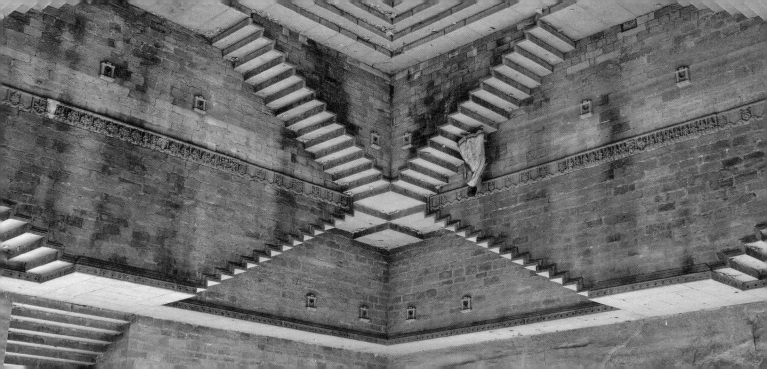

Climbing up from the depths of the Ramkund stepwell. Located in Bhuj, in India's Gujarat state, Ramkund is square-shaped and geometrically precise but is decorated with miniature idols inspired by the Ramayana.

PHOTO: TUUL & BRUNO MORANDI

| 17 Monday ☾ | 18 Tuesday | 19 Wednesday | 20 Thursday | 21 Friday | 22 Saturday | 23 Sunday |

OCTOBER

WEEK 42

Stairs are your teacher; they teach you to be stronger. Love your teacher and every time life puts some stairs before you, accept them as a present!
MEHMET MURAT İLDAN Turkish writer (1965-)

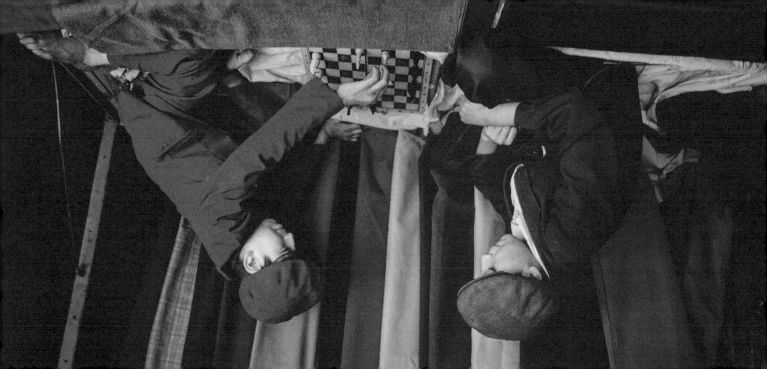

Young Uyghur boys playing chess in the fabric bazaar of Kashgar old town in Xinjiang Province, China. Chess is still much less popular in China than *xiangqi* (Chinese chess) and *weiqi* (go).

OCTOBER

24 Monday
DIWALI (HINDU, SIKH),
LABOUR DAY (NZ)

25 Tuesday ☺

26 Wednesday

27 Thursday

28 Friday

29 Saturday

30 Sunday
CLOCKS CHANGE
(EUROPE)

WEEK 43

It only takes a mistake to lose the game, while it takes an ingenious plan to win one.
CHINESE SAYING (actually about the game *xiangqi*)

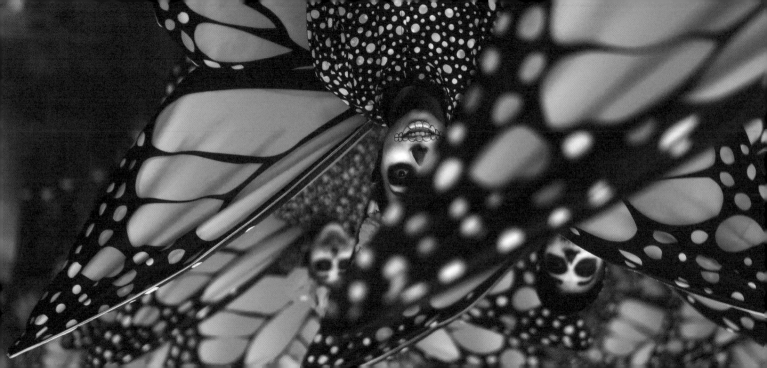

A riot of colour and life to welcome back the souls of departed relatives. Participants dressed as monarch butterflies perform during Mexico City's annual Day of the Dead parade in 2019.

PHOTO: GUSTAVO GRAF/REUTERS

31 Monday	1 Tuesday ☽	2 Wednesday	3 Thursday	4 Friday	5 Saturday	6 Sunday
HALLOWEEN SAMHAIN (PAGAN)		DAY OF THE DEAD				CLOCKS CHANGE (CAN/US)

OCTOBER

NOVEMBER

WEEK 44

As long as we remember those who have passed away, as long as we tell their stories, sing their songs, tell their jokes, cook their favourite meals, then they are with us, around us, and in our hearts. The moment we forget them... then they are truly gone.
JORGE R GUTIERREZ Mexican animator, painter and writer (1975-)

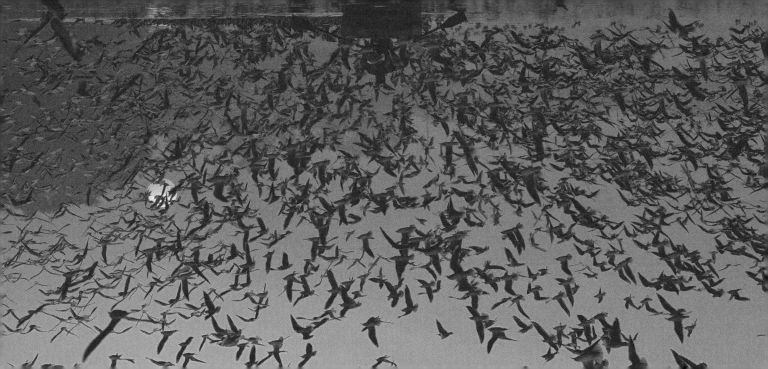

Seagulls explode into the air as a boat is propelled across the River Yamuna at dawn in New Delhi, India. The Yamuna flows 1,376 kilometres from the Lower Himalaya to meet the Ganges at Triveni Sangam.

PHOTO: ANUSHREE FADNAVIS/REUTERS

NOVEMBER

7 Monday	8 Tuesday ☺	9 Wednesday	10 Thursday	11 Friday	12 Saturday	13 Sunday

11 Friday
VETERANS' DAY (US);
REMEMBRANCE DAY (CAN)

WEEK 45

Birds were created to record everything. They were not designed just to be beautiful jewels in the sky, but to serve as the eyes of heaven.
SUZY KASSEM Egyptian-American artist (1975-)

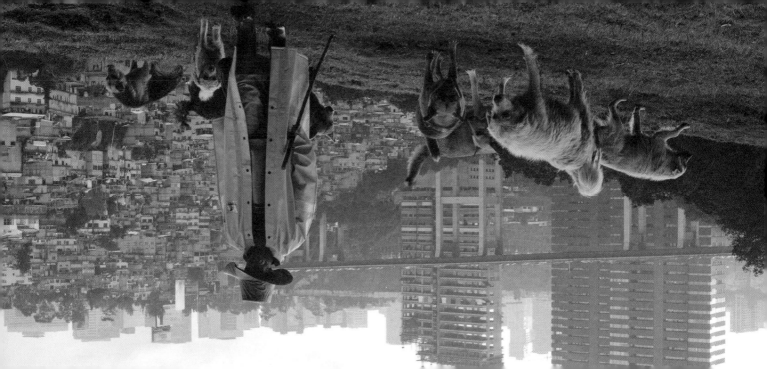

Gerardo Carmona walks with his dogs on a grassy hill in the district of Santa Fe with the vastness of Mexico City sprawling beneath him. The world's fifth-largest megacity, it has a population of over 21 million.

PHOTO: LUIS ANTONIO ROJAS/PANOS

14 Monday	15 Tuesday	16 Wednesday ☾	17 Thursday	18 Friday	19 Saturday	20 Sunday

NOVEMBER

WEEK 46

I live through risk. Without risk there is no art. You should always be on the edge of a cliff about to fall down and break your neck.
CARLOS FUENTES Mexican writer (1928-2012)

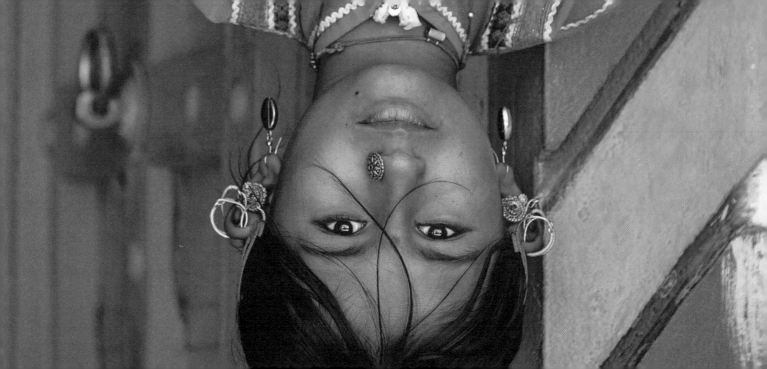

A girl in front of her house in Hodka village, in the Indian state of Gujarat. She comes from the Meghwal people, who claim descent from Rishi Megh, a saint who brought rain from the clouds through prayer.

PHOTO: TUUL & BRUNO MORANDI

NOVEMBER

21 Monday	22 Tuesday	23 Wednesday ●	24 Thursday	25 Friday	26 Saturday	27 Sunday
			THANKSGIVING (US)			FIRST SUNDAY OF ADVENT (CHRISTIAN)

WEEK 47

To every child – I dream of a world where you can laugh, dance, sing, learn, live in peace and be happy.
MALALA YOUSAFZAI Pakistani activist (1997-)

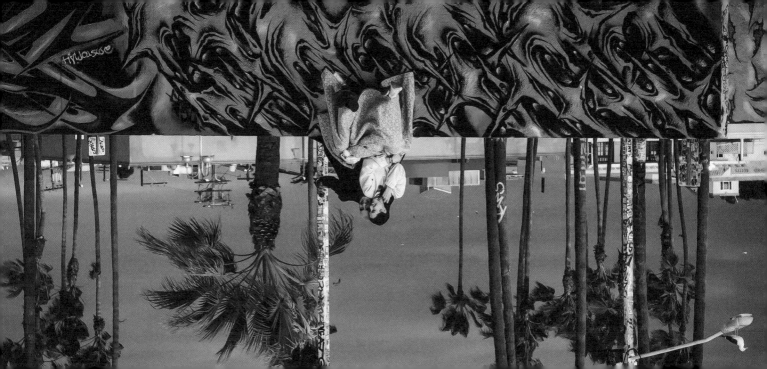

Here's looking at us – a couple takes a selfie at sunset on Venice Beach. The seaside town was absorbed by Los Angeles in 1926 but retains a bohemian character with quirky shops and mural art.

PHOTO: DINA LITOVSKY

28 Monday	29 Tuesday	30 Wednesday ☽	1 Thursday	2 Friday	3 Saturday	4 Sunday
			WORLD AIDS DAY			

NOVEMBER

DECEMBER

WEEK 48

A selfie has more face and fewer feelings.
AMIT KALANTRI Indian author (1988-)

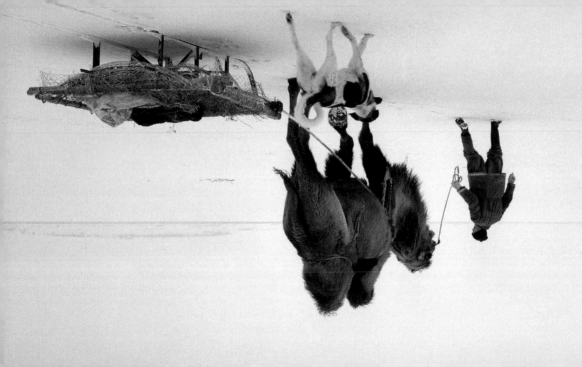

A fisher leads his camel through the snow, pulling a sledge towards his fishing spot in the Aral Sea, just a few kilometres from their home village of Tastubek, in Kazakhstan.

PHOTO: LAURENT WEYL/PANOS

5 Monday	**6** Tuesday	**7** Wednesday	**8** Thursday ☺	**9** Friday	**10** Saturday	**11** Sunday

DECEMBER

WEEK 49

The difference between camels and men: a camel can work a week and not drink; a man can drink a week and not work.
JULIAN TUWIM Polish poet (1894-1953)

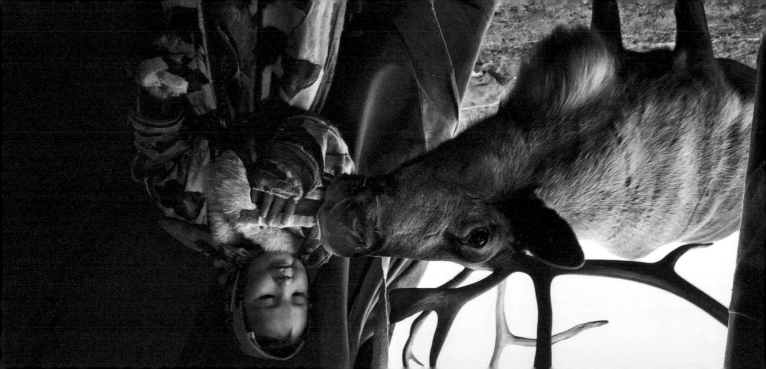

A snack for my sister. The reindeer poking her nose through six-year-old Angelica's tent door is not just part of the family herd but has a special status. The family are from the Nenets people in Siberia, Russia. ◆

12 Monday

13 Tuesday

14 Wednesday

15 Thursday

16 Friday ☾

17 Saturday

18 Sunday

HANUKKAH BEGINS
(JEWISH)

DECEMBER

WEEK 50

Animals are such agreeable friends – they ask no questions, they pass no criticisms.
GEORGE ELIOT/MARY ANN EVANS British writer (1819-80)

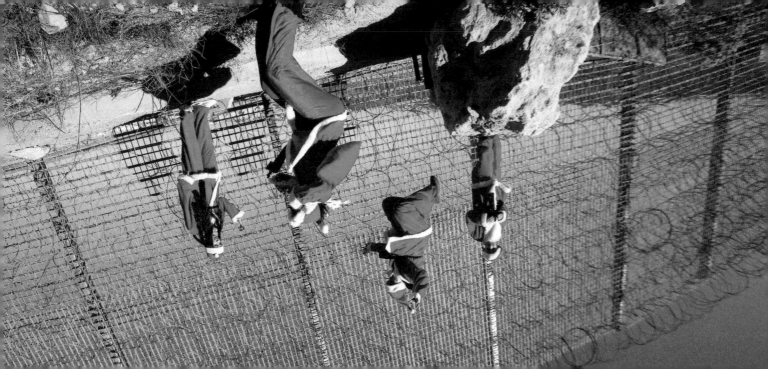

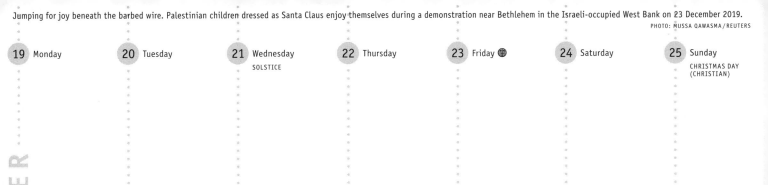

Jumping for joy beneath the barbed wire. Palestinian children dressed as Santa Claus enjoy themselves during a demonstration near Bethlehem in the Israeli-occupied West Bank on 23 December 2019.

19 Monday

20 Tuesday

21 Wednesday
SOLSTICE

22 Thursday

23 Friday ⏺

24 Saturday

25 Sunday
CHRISTMAS DAY
(CHRISTIAN)

DECEMBER

We have the right to refuse. This is our right, yours and mine. You can't know all the laws by heart,
you don't know what will happen if you refuse. But you have to try.
MARIA ALYOKHINA, Russian musician and activist (1988-)

WEEK 51

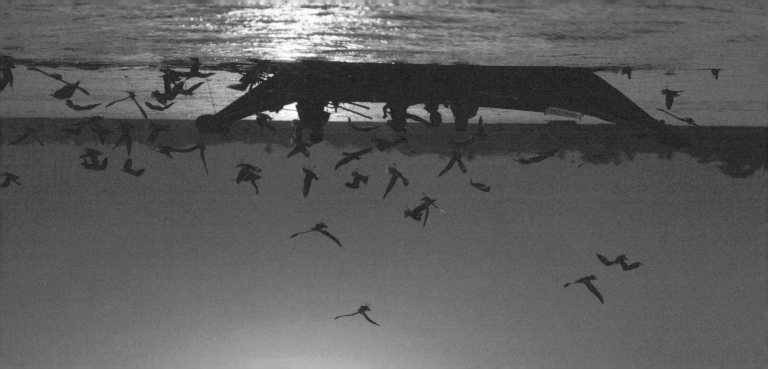

Sunset over the river in Yangon, Myanmar's biggest city, as birds are drawn inexorably to the possibility of food. Yangon was the capital until 2005 when the country's military rulers switched this to Naypyidaw.

DECEMBER

26 Monday	27 Tuesday	28 Wednesday	29 Thursday	30 Friday ☽	31 Saturday	1 Sunday
PUBLIC HOLIDAY (AUS, CAN, NZ, UK)	PUBLIC HOLIDAY (AUS, CAN, NZ, UK)					NEW YEAR'S DAY

JANUARY

WEEK 52

A strip of water's spread in the setting sun/ Half the river's emerald, half is red.
BAI JUYI Chinese poet (772-846)

JANUARY

1	**SUN**
2	MON
3	TUE
4	WED
5	THU
6	FRI
7	SAT
8	**SUN**
9	MON
10	TUE
11	WED
12	THU
13	FRI
14	SAT
15	**SUN**
16	MON
17	TUE
18	WED
19	THU
20	FRI
21	SAT
22	**SUN**
23	MON
24	TUE
25	WED
26	THU
27	FRI
28	SAT
29	**SUN**
30	MON
31	TUE

FEBRUARY

1	WED
2	THU
3	FRI
4	SAT
5	**SUN**
6	MON
7	TUE
8	WED
9	THU
10	FRI
11	SAT
12	**SUN**
13	MON
14	TUE
15	WED
16	THU
17	FRI
18	SAT
19	**SUN**
20	MON
21	TUE
22	WED
23	THU
24	FRI
25	SAT
26	**SUN**
27	MON
28	TUE

MARCH

1	WED
2	THU
3	FRI
4	SAT
5	**SUN**
6	MON
7	TUE
8	WED
9	THU
10	FRI
11	SAT
12	**SUN**
13	MON
14	TUE
15	WED
16	THU
17	FRI
18	SAT
19	**SUN**
20	MON
21	TUE
22	WED
23	THU
24	FRI
25	SAT
26	**SUN**
27	MON
28	TUE
29	WED
30	THU
31	FRI

APRIL

1	SAT
2	**SUN**
3	MON
4	TUE
5	WED
6	THU
7	FRI
8	SAT
9	**SUN**
10	MON
11	TUE
12	WED
13	THU
14	FRI
15	SAT
16	**SUN**
17	MON
18	TUE
19	WED
20	THU
21	FRI
22	SAT
23	**SUN**
24	MON
25	TUE
26	WED
27	THU
28	FRI
29	SAT
30	**SUN**

MAY	JUNE	JULY	AUGUST
1 MON	1 THU	1 SAT	1 TUE
2 TUE	2 FRI	**2 SUN**	**2 WED**
3 WED	3 SAT	3 MON	3 THU
4 THU	**4 SUN**	4 TUE	4 FRI
5 FRI	5 MON	5 WED	5 SAT
6 SAT	6 TUE	6 THU	**6 SUN**
7 SUN	7 WED	7 FRI	7 MON
8 MON	8 THU	8 SAT	8 TUE
9 TUE	9 FRI	**9 SUN**	9 WED
10 WED	10 SAT	10 MON	10 THU
11 THU	**11 SUN**	11 TUE	11 FRI
12 FRI	12 MON	12 WED	12 SAT
13 SAT	13 TUE	13 THU	**13 SUN**
14 SUN	14 WED	14 FRI	14 MON
15 MON	15 THU	15 SAT	15 TUE
16 TUE	16 FRI	**16 SUN**	16 WED
17 WED	17 SAT	17 MON	17 THU
18 THU	**18 SUN**	18 TUE	18 FRI
19 FRI	19 MON	19 WED	19 SAT
20 SAT	20 TUE	20 THU	**20 SUN**
21 SUN	21 WED	21 FRI	21 MON
22 MON	22 THU	22 SAT	22 TUE
23 TUE	23 FRI	**23 SUN**	23 WED
24 WED	24 SAT	24 MON	24 THU
25 THU	**25 SUN**	25 TUE	25 FRI
26 FRI	26 MON	26 WED	26 SAT
27 SAT	27 TUE	27 THU	**27 SUN**
28 SUN	28 WED	28 FRI	28 MON
29 MON	29 THU	29 SAT	29 TUE
30 TUE	30 FRI	**30 SUN**	30 WED
31 WED		31 MON	31 THU

2023

DECEMBER	NOVEMBER	OCTOBER	SEPTEMBER
31 SUN	30 THU	31 TUE	30 SAT
30 SAT	29 WED	30 MON	29 FRI
29 FRI	28 TUE	29 SUN	28 THU
28 THU	27 MON	28 SAT	27 WED
27 WED	26 SUN	27 FRI	26 TUE
26 TUE	25 SAT	26 THU	25 MON
25 MON	24 FRI	25 WED	24 SUN
24 SUN	23 THU	24 TUE	23 SAT
23 SAT	22 WED	23 MON	22 FRI
22 FRI	21 TUE	22 SUN	21 THU
21 THU	20 MON	21 SAT	20 WED
20 WED	19 SUN	20 FRI	19 TUE
19 TUE	18 SAT	19 THU	18 MON
18 MON	17 FRI	18 WED	17 SUN
17 SUN	16 THU	17 TUE	16 SAT
16 SAT	15 WED	16 MON	15 FRI
15 FRI	14 TUE	15 SUN	14 THU
14 THU	13 MON	14 SAT	13 WED
13 WED	12 SUN	13 FRI	12 TUE
12 TUE	11 SAT	12 THU	11 MON
11 MON	10 FRI	11 WED	10 SUN
10 SUN	9 THU	10 TUE	9 SAT
9 SAT	8 WED	9 MON	8 FRI
8 FRI	7 TUE	8 SUN	7 THU
7 THU	6 MON	7 SAT	6 WED
6 WED	5 SUN	6 FRI	5 TUE
5 TUE	4 SAT	5 THU	4 MON
4 MON	3 FRI	4 WED	3 SUN
3 SUN	2 THU	3 TUE	2 SAT
2 SAT	1 WED	2 MON	1 FRI
1 FRI		1 SUN	

3 2 0 2

In depth

More background on some of the Almanac photographs.

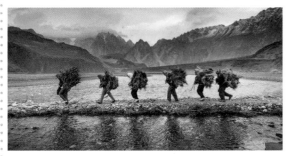

THE KEY TO SURVIVAL WEEK 52

Photographer Matthieu Paley writes:
I am on a wood-gathering mission with women who must be my grandmother's age – Zamrad Begum and Nasib Sultan. This is going to be a workout all right – and these two are fit as hell!

We climb up on the far side of the river, reaching Zor Abad, a quiet orchard in its winter slumber. Zamrad grabs the thorny branches with her bare hands and piles them up high, tying them with a rope. Nasib laughs, 'Dear Zamrad, such a beautiful thing you are doing, a nice bundle, a real jewel, like your necklace!'

After another 30 minutes of hard work, they run down the mountain, loaded with wood, meeting up with other women, daughters and grand-daughters. All the way home they chat between bouts of laughter, making fun of the village men, singing songs about 'Bulbul', the famous nightingale. I puff along behind, eating their dust.

We walk into Zamrad's home, passing a sleepy donkey. People gather around the *dildung*, the central fireplace, and I am asked to sit by the *loop raj*, the honorific place near the fire, away from the door. Fading light falls gently on the women from an opening in the roof. With the rasp of a match striking and a couple of gentle blows, the first flames light up the house.

'See, fire is where it all starts, it's the way to the stomach.' Zamrad sits on the floor, next to me. 'In this season, we eat a lot of *shhikerkutz hoi* (potatoes mixed with fenugreek). And no meal goes without chapati, our daily bread.'

'And where do all these vegetables come from?' I ask.

Zamrad points to a side of the house. 'Behind that wall, from our field, where else?' I've heard it said the enemy of food is miles. Here, proximity is the key to survival.

CHINESE YEAR OF THE TIGER

The Chinese lunar calendar is the oldest of time records, dating back to 2637 BCE. A complete cycle takes 60 years and is made up of five simple cycles of 12, each year being represented by an animal. The animal ruling in the year you were born is supposed to have a great influence on your life. Other years of the tiger were 1902, 1914, 1926, 1938, 1950, 1962, 1974, 1986, 1998, 2010.

- Chinese name for the tiger: Hu
- Hours ruled by the tiger: 3 am to 5 am
- Direction of its sign: East
- Season and principal month: Winter, February
- Astrological house: Expansion

In Chinese astrology the tiger is characterized as being fearless, unflinching and rash. The tiger personality has an unrestrainable passion to compete but, with its positive features being magnetism and attractiveness, it stands a better chance than most. People born in this year have an iron fist hidden inside their velvet glove. Other traits of the tiger personality are pride, immediate vengefulness and unpredictability.

Famous people born in the year of the tiger: Fidel Castro, Marilyn Monroe, Penelope Cruz, Emily Brontë, Issey Miyake, Emily Dickinson, Roberta Flack, Octavio Paz, Marguerite Duras, Julie Walters, David Attenborough, Agatha Christie, Marie Curie, Sun Ra, Tove Jansson, Miles Davis, Fela Kuti, Liv Ullmann.

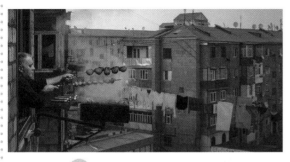

BBQ CITY
WEEK 14

'The two things that define our culture are mulberry vodka and barbecues,' says David Abgaryan, who is shown in the photograph cooking dinner outside the window of his fourth-floor apartment in Stepanakert.

Buildings in this city often have small communal barbecues. For those who live in buildings without a shared grill, many residents install a home-made version that swings outside of their window alongside washing lines full of clothes.

'Like many people in town,' says David, 'we don't have a house with a yard, so this is how we grill. Someone came up with the idea about 20 years ago and it just stuck. You can find these all over town. I cook on mine all the time.'

Stepanakert has a troubled history and a potentially explosive present. It is the capital of the de facto republic of Artsakh, which is not recognized by the United Nations and is considered to be part of Azerbaijan, though its people are almost entirely Armenian. Artsakh was once known as Nagorno-Karabakh and was at the heart of a bitter war that erupted amid the disintegration of the Soviet Union in the early 1990s – few are the buildings in Stepanakert that were not damaged during the war.

In 2020 conflict between Armenia and Azerbaijan over the disputed territory erupted again. Both sides imposed martial law and mobilized troops, and thousands of lives were lost in fighting over the ensuing months. Buildings and communities in Stepanakert once again suffered bombardment.

RHAPSODY IN BLUE

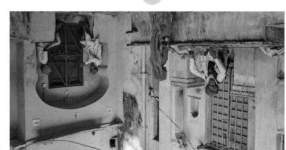

Jodhpur, the second city of the Indian state of Rajasthan, is famous for two things – the blue colour of its buildings and its food.

Not all the city's buildings have the same colour; only those in the old town nestling at the foot of the Mehrangarh fortress. But their particular shade of blue is spectacular. The reason for the colour is, however, disputed. Some maintain that the houses were originally painted this way by devotees of Shiva – legend has it that the god ingested a poison that turned his body blue in order to save the planet. Others maintain this was a colour associated with the Brahmin, or priestly, caste. Still others contend that a paint containing copper sulphate and lime-stone was used in order to deter termites that were damaging many historic buildings in the city. Meanwhile

there are those locals who believe that blue reflects the sun's rays and thus keeps the houses cool.

Among the Jodhpur foodstuffs that are celebrated throughout India are: *mirchi bada*, a spicy snack based on banana pepper, chilli, potato and cauli-flower stuffing, usually served hot with tomato sauce; *mawa kachori*, a fried dumpling filled with dried milk and nuts, and coated in aromatic syrup; *makhaniya lassi*, a dairy drink with dollops of butter floating in it that can be garnished with nuts, pomegranate seeds or saffron; and *Jodhpuri gulab jamun ki sabzi*, where the milk-based sweets are deep fried and dipped in a tomato and cashew-nut gravy. There are sweet shops throughout India called 'Jodhpur Sweets' – testimony to the city's culinary fame.

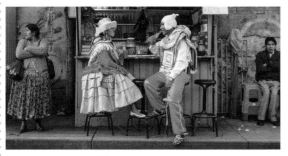

DANCE BREAK

The couple in this photograph – Wilma Canchi and Raul Limachi – have only stopped for a refreshing cold drink but this roadside kiosk in the Bolivian city of La Paz offers more than just coffees, teas and juices. The signs promote its chicken soup, chicken stew and its *caldo de panza pata* – a broth made from a cow's intestines and hooves.

Other popular Bolivian street foods include *llauchas* (cheese pasties), *salteñas* (baked pasties filled with meat, spices, potatoes, eggs and olives), *api* (a purple maize drink often served with fritters called *buñuelos*) and *pasankallas* (a sugary version of popcorn).

Wilma and Raul are much more elaborately and colourfully dressed than the people around them because they are performers in the Kullawada dance. This celebrates the traditional weavers of alpaca wool from among the Aymara people of the Andes and is thought to date from the heyday of the Inca empire, which was at its peak in the 15th century.

The dance was suppressed during colonial times because it was considered idolatrous but has become increasingly popular, not least as part of the many folk festivals celebrated in La Paz – the capital is said to host around 800 per year.

The most important of these festivals is the Fiesta del Gran Poder ('Great Power' – a reference to Jesus Christ), in late May or early June, in which around 30,000 dancers parade along the six-kilometre route for 12 hours wearing elaborate handmade costumes that symbolize key events in Bolivian and indigenous history.

SALT AND THE ROSE LAKE

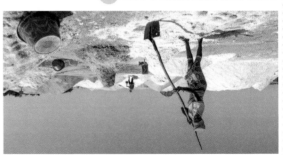

Harvesting salt for use in cooking and as a condiment is a time-honoured practice in many parts of the world. Salt lakes form in closed or semi-enclosed basins where the mineral content is naturally high in salinity and where drought conditions are common. Among the most celebrated of these are the Dead Sea in Palestine, Lake Chad in North Africa, Lake Chaerhan in China and the Great Salt Lake in the US.

Lake Retba (or Lac Rose) in the West African state of Senegal, where the salt in this photograph is being gathered, is also famous – but not so much for its white salt as for the pink colour of its water, which is particularly startling when seen from the air during the dry season from November to June. This pink tinge derives from the

algae *Dunaliella salina*, which produces a red pigment that enables it better to absorb light and create energy. The composer Michael Tippett was inspired by the sight of it to write 'The Rose Lake', the penultimate piece he wrote before his death in 1998. The sand dunes that separate the lake from the Atlantic Ocean have a distinctly terracotta hue.

The lake's waters have around one-third salt content, comparable to the Dead Sea – the normal saline content of sea water, by contrast, is only 3.5 per cent. The salt is gathered from it by around 3,000 workers, who protect their skin while working by smearing it with shea butter. Senegalese fisherfolk use the salt to preserve fish, not least for the national dish, *thieboudienne*.

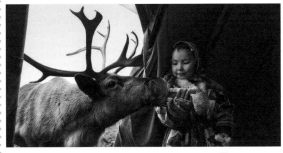

GUESS WHO'S COMING TO DINNER WEEK 50

Six-year-old Angelica belongs to the Nenets people of northern Siberia. The reindeer, originally an orphan, belongs to her family and is used to sticking her nose in through the entrance of the tent or *chum* and being rewarded with a piece of dry bread. Every Nenets family owns a sacred reindeer that must not be used to tow the sleigh or be killed.

The Nenets – the name simply means 'human' in their language – have a symbiotic relationship with their reindeer in more ways than this. They depend on the animals for food and the skins that provide their clothing and their tents. And since time immemorial they have moved with their reindeer herds in search of good lichen pasture according to the seasons – southwards in winter to the shelter of the taiga forests and northwards in summer to an Arctic peninsula stretching out into the Kara Sea. This apparently desolate place is their homeland, which they call *Ya-Mal* – the end of the world.

The Nenets' annual migratory round trip is 1,100 kilometres long and is generally undertaken using wooden sleds that work better on snow than on the open ground. These days, though, some are to be found using both motorized sleds and mobile phones. These modern items are most likely to be funded from the sale of reindeer antlers into the Chinese market. Antlers are shed by the animals each year as a matter of course and the velvety interior of them is greatly valued in China, not least as an aphrodisiac.

Number nuggets

3.4 million – the number of emails sent in the world every second. This compares with 741,000 WhatsApp messages per second, 69,000 Google searches per second and 55,000 Facebook posts per second.

1 million – the estimated number of animal and plant species threatened with extinction, including 1 in 3 freshwater species and 2 in 5 plants.

19% – the proportion of people in Africa who go hungry – around 250 million people.

1 in 3 – the proportion of the world's children under 5 who were either stunted (too short) or wasted (too thin) in 2019, 98% of whom live in low- and middle-income countries.

1 in 3 – coincidentally this is also the proportion of people worldwide who are overweight or obese.

$218 billion – the amount spent in the US every year on growing, processing, transporting and disposing of food that is never eaten.

960,000 – the number of times the fake news that the Pope was endorsing Trump was shared during the 2016 US election.

$721 billion – the combined fines and pay-outs awarded against Google between 2018 and 2020 for breaching privacy and data-protection laws, breaking anti-trust rules and preventing rivals from competing fairly.

6,000 – the number of satellites currently orbiting the Earth, 60% of which are now non-functional junk.

159 – the number of countries that can be visited by a German citizen without a visa.

22 – the number of countries that can be visited by an Afghan citizen without a visa.

$95.7 billion – the amount spent on pets in the US in 2019.

6 – the number of times faster that false news on Twitter spreads compared with accurate information.

3 million – the annual number of deaths attributable to ambient air pollution.

4.3 million – the annual number of deaths attributable to household air pollution.

3 years – life expectancy lost globally due to air pollution.

8.8 kilograms – the average amount of chocolate consumed each year by someone in Switzerland, the world's most chocoholic country. Austria and Germany come close behind.

$1,917 billion – world military expenditure in 2019. The US was responsible for 38% of this and China for 14%.

1st – Iceland's ranking in the 2020 Global Peace Index. Afghanistan was the world's least peaceful country, with Syria next.

121st – the US's ranking out of 163 countries rated in the 2020 Global Peace Index – below, for example, Haiti, Honduras and Algeria.

$197 billion – the fortune of Elon Musk, the world's richest individual as of January 2021.

90% – the proportion of the global soybean crop grown to feed animals for the meat industry; only 6% of soya is eaten directly by humans.

13.8 billion – the number of years some photons of microwave radiation have taken to reach Earth from the farthest reach of the observable universe.

200 billion – the estimated number of stars in our own galaxy, the Milky Way, which is itself just one of an estimated 200 billion such galaxies.

250 million – the estimated number of participants in India's General Strike in November 2020, protesting against the government's farming reforms.

320 million – the number of Facebook users in India, surpassing by far the 190 million in the US.

BIODIVERSITY LOSS AND HOW TO REVERSE IT

What's causing it?

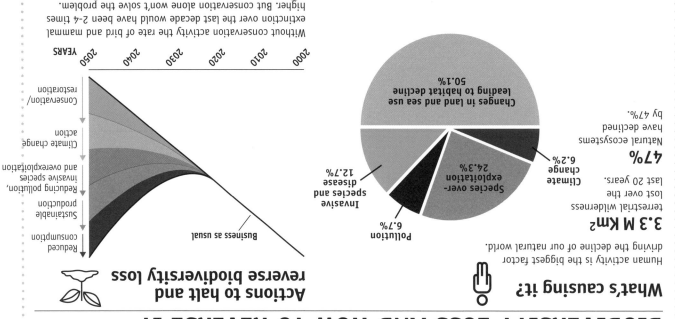

Human activity is the biggest factor driving the decline of our natural world.

3.3 M Km²
terrestrial wilderness lost over the last 20 years.

47%
Natural ecosystems have declined by 47%.

Changes in land and sea use leading to habitat decline 50.1%

Species over-exploitation 24.3%

Invasive species and disease 12.7%

Pollution 6.7%

Climate change 6.2%

Actions to halt and reverse biodiversity loss

Business as usual

Reduced consumption
Sustainable production
Reducing pollution, invasive species and overexploitation
Climate change action
Conservation/ restoration

YEARS
2000 2010 2020 2030 2040 2050

Without conservation activity the rate of bird and mammal extinction over the last decade would have been 2–4 times higher. But conservation alone won't solve the problem.

Last thought...

'We chose to risk new paths to achieve greater happiness. We chose to apply new techniques and to look for forms of organization better suited to our civilization. We abruptly and definitively rejected all forms of foreign diktats, thus creating the conditions for a dignity worthy of our ambitions. To reject mere survival and ease the pressures; to liberate the countryside from feudal paralysis or regression; to democratize our society and open our minds to a universe of collective responsibility in order to dare to invent the future.'

THOMAS SANKARA
Burkina Faso's revolutionary leader
(1949-87)

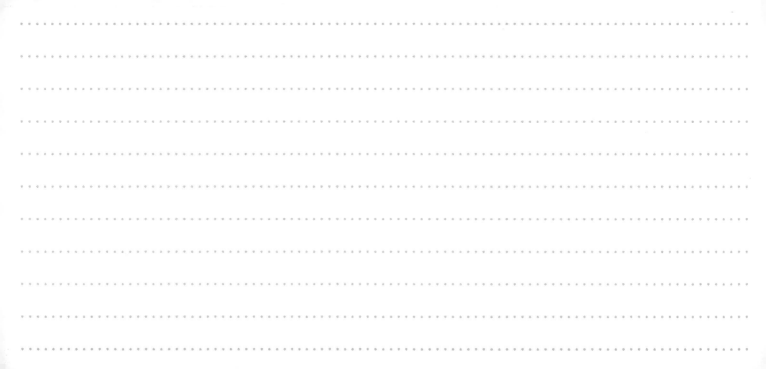

About New Internationalist

New Internationalist is a leading independent media organization dedicated to socially conscious journalism and publishing. We are proud to be a multi-stakeholder co-operative co-owned by our workers and over 4,000 investors. Our aim is to inform, inspire and empower people to build a fairer, more sustainable planet. We publish a global justice magazine and a range of publications.

Magazine

The New Internationalist magazine has reported on human rights, social and environmental justice for more than four decades. Our journalism aims to shine a light on the people whose struggles otherwise tend to go unseen and unheard.

newint.org/

Ethical Mail Order

We run the Ethical Shop in the UK. Besides selling our branded publications and products, we specialize in sourcing and marketing useful, fair trade, eco-friendly, organic and educational gift items.

ethicalshop.org/

newint.org

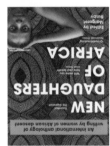

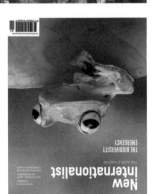

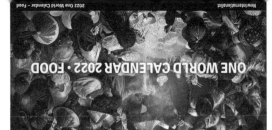